Creative Plans For
YARD & GARDEN
STRUCTURES

Design G217

42 Easy-To-Build Designs For Gazebos, Sheds, Pool Houses, Playsets, Bridges and More!

Designs by
Matt DeBacker, Designer

Project Manager
Marlin Pritchard

Written by
Connie Brown

HOME PLANNERS, INC.
3275 West Ina Road, Suite 110, Tucson, AZ 85741

Contents

Book Design by:
  Paul Fitzgerald, graphic designer
  Kellie Gibson, graphic designer

Photographs:
Front Cover:
©Werner G. Bertsch/Fotoconcept, Inc.
Back Cover:
©Frank Oberle/Photographic
  Resources, Inc.

Published by Home Planners, Inc.
  Editorial and Corporate Offices:
    3275 West Ina Road, Suite 110
    Tucson, Arizona 85741
  Distribution Center:
    29333 Lorie Lane
    Wixom, Michigan 48393

President and Publisher:
  Rickard D. Bailey
Publications Manager:
  Cindy J. Coatsworth
Senior Editor: Paulette Mulvin

Library of Congress
Catalogue Card Number: 94-079099

ISBN: 1-881955-20-6

10 9 8 7 6 5 4 3 2 1

On The Cover: This romantic gazebo
will be the delight of your backyard
parties. Finish as shown for a delicate
Victorian look or use more rustic materials for an entirely different effect.
For more information, see page 12.

Building Basics for Yard and Garden
          Structures 3
Yard and Garden Structures 11
    Gazebos 12
    Lawn Sheds 30
    Compost Bin (with Complete
          Building Instructions) 44
    Playhouses 46
    Studios and Cottages 54
    Playsets 62
    Cabanas and Pavillions 70
    Trellises 76
    Swings, Strombellas and Arbors 84
    Bridges 90
Ordering Blueprints for Plans in This Book . . 92
Index and Order Form 94
Useful Finishing Sources 96

Building Basics

For Yard and Garden Structures

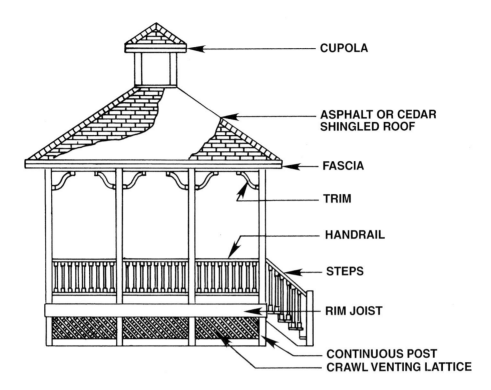

- CUPOLA
- ASPHALT OR CEDAR SHINGLED ROOF
- FASCIA
- TRIM
- HANDRAIL
- STEPS
- RIM JOIST
- CONTINUOUS POST
- CRAWL VENTING LATTICE

I magine . . . a playhouse for your children just outside your kitchen window; or your very own, free-standing shed for gardening or craft tools and supplies; or, a lovely garden swing nestled in a se-cluded, shady area by the side of your house. Or, on a more practical note, would your yard benefit from a compost bin, a pool cabana, or a bridge over a rocky or marshy area that is always such a problem?

Decorative, functional or just for fun, amenities and refinements *outside* your home can increase its living area and value—and provide hours of safe, relaxing outdoor living for every member of your family.

Projects such as those in this book are very do-able! With an understanding of the basics, the right tools for the job, a set of our plans—plus an adequate supply of time and patience—you can turn a corner of your yard or garden into a useful and practical work area, or a charming and restful hideaway.

ADVANCE PLANNING
Project Selection

The first step, of course, is to decide on the project. Of all the possibilities, what does your home, your property, your family need the most: a garden swing, a children's playset, a whimsical gazebo, or a practical tool shed?

If you already know what outdoor structure you want to add to your property (a lawn shed for garden supplies and equipment, perhaps) then move right along to the next easy step. Simply select the size and layout you prefer from the 7 plans for lawn sheds shown in this book. Then turn to page 92 for order information, and you're on your way.

> *Remember, well-thought-out advance planning is crucial to a successful project.*

Sometimes deciding what to build is not so easy. Keeping in mind the available space on your property and your budget, look through this book for ideas. The detailed descriptions of a wide variety of outdoor struc-tures on pages 12-91 are sure to spark your imagination. Many designs have a variety of options, some just tailor-made for your family.

With all the possibilities fresh in your mind, take a slow walk around your property and decide which of the outdoor structures is the best match in form and function to your family's needs and the space and budget you have available.

You'll need to consider if you have the time and expertise to build the project you've selected, or if you will need to involve a licensed contractor for all or part of the work.

Once all that's decided, refer to page 92 to order the plans you need and turn your thoughts to site selection.

Site Selection

Site selection depends on a number of things: what you are building, its purpose, who is going to use it, its accessibility, and its appeal.

Location: If you decide to build a gazebo, it will likely become the focal point of your property. If you are constructing a playset, select an area that is visible from the house so you can watch the children. And, if your project is a compost bin, you probably want it located to the rear or side of your property, out of sight.

Drainage: If your property has moist areas, avoid them if you can. Don't place a playset or a garden swing in an area that remains damp for two or three days after a rain. The alternative is to provide a dry, firm base by adding sand and gravel fill under the project to aid the drainage of the site.

Utilities: Plan ahead for any utilities your project may require: electricity or water for sheds, gazebos and playhouses, or gas for heat or a grill. **Call your local utilities providers for locations of underground cable and water lines, if necessary.**

BUILDING BASICS

Building Permits

When your advance planning and site selection are complete, it's time to obtain the required building permits. Separate building permits are usually needed for each construction discipline: one for the structure, one for the electrical work, one for the plumbing, one for the heating, and so on. Specific requirements for each vary from region to region across the country. Check with your local building officials *before you begin your project* to determine which permits you need. If your project is small, permits may not be required.

> Check with your local building officials *before you begin your project* to determine which permits you need.

Building Codes

Along with building permits come the codes which must be met. These codes are usually imposed by county or city governments. Codes are required to ensure that your project meets all standards for safety and construction methods. A local inspector will usually

check the progress of your project at various stages, and there could be more than one inspector, depending on the utilities you incorporate.

Some of the regulated items the inspectors will check include: distance of project from property lines, handrail heights, stair construction, connection methods, footing sizes and depths, material being used, plumbing, electrical and mechanical requirements and neighborhood zoning regulations.

Site Plan

Creating a site plan, or detailed layout of the project on the property, is important when incorporating a new addition to an existing landscape. A site plan allows you to view in advance the effect a new structure will have when finished. It is important to conceptualize how the new addition blends in with property lines, utilities, other structures, permanent mature plants, land contours and roads. You also need to be certain of the visibility of the new structure from vantage points both outside and within your property lines. In addition, a site plan may be required by local building officials.

Tools Checklist

If you are an experienced do-it-yourselfer, you probably have most of the tools needed for any of the projects in this book. If this is your first project, compare the tools you have on hand to the list below. Most are available at rental shops, so you can have "the right tool for the job" without spending a lot of extra money right at first.

Gather together the tools you will need for your project *before you begin construction*. This simple rule is as important as having your building materials and lumber on site in the needed sizes and quantity before you start. The frustration and aggravation you eliminate will be well worth the time it takes to get organized before you begin.

Your basic tool list should include:

Brushes and rollers to apply finishes	Plumb bob
	Power drill and screwdriver
Carpenter's level	Power jigsaw
Carpenter's square	Shovel
Chalk line	Socket set
Chisel	Tape measure
Circular saw	Tool belt
Framing angle	Line level
Hammer	Nail set
Handsaw	Wheelbarrow (to move materials and to mix concrete)

Selecting Lumber

Each project in this book has a list of lumber and other building materials required. You will need to determine and select the type of wood you want to use. Many wood species are used for outdoor structures. Among the most common are: Redwood, Western Red

Cedar, Douglas Fir, Spruce, Southern Yellow Pine, Northern Pine and Ponderosa Pine.

Lumber is available in a variety of grades depending on quality, strength and resistance to decay. For example, Redwood is graded as follows (listed from highest to lowest quality): Clear All Heart, Select Heart, Construction Heart and Merchantable Heart. Any of the last three grades are commonly used in outdoor construction projects.

One of the primary considerations in selecting the correct lumber for your project is to prevent the base structure from decaying. For this reason, lumber that is in contact with, or even in close proximity to, the ground must be decay-resistant. Select a resistant species and treat your lumber with a preservative before using it in your building or project.

> *Because of the chemicals used in its treatment, pressure-treated wood should not be used if it will come into direct contact with drinking water or food for humans or animals.*

You might want to select pressure-treated wood, which is available from most lumber dealers and home centers. In pressure-treated wood, preservatives or fire-retardant chemicals are forced into the fibers of the lumber to protect and prolong its durability. Although pressure-treated wood seems an obvious choice, some precautions and decisions about its use are warranted. *Because of the chemicals used in its treatment, pressure-treated wood should not be used if it will come into direct contact with drinking water or food for humans or animals.* Further precautions include: do not use boards with a visible chemical residue; wear a mask and goggles when sawing treated wood; do not burn treated wood; and sweep up and safely dispose of all sawdust and wood scraps. Check with your lumber supplier for additional restrictions and precautions.

Choose a lumber dealer you can rely on to assist you with wood selection—one who will be familiar with the lumber commonly used in your area for outdoor projects. Be sure what you want is available locally. If you desire a wood type that is not normally in stock in your part of the country, you'll pay much more to acquire it.

SITE PREPARATION

At last, it's time to begin! You've selected the site according to your observations and site plan; you've obtained complete project plans; you've secured all permits; and you've gathered together all code-approved materials and required tools. Now, to help assure success, follow these important steps so construction will proceed quickly and without too many hitches.

Drainage: This is an important word to remember when you begin construction. Water must drain away from the foundation or it will pool on structural supports, eventually rotting and weakening them. And, water-saturated soil beneath footings may not remain firm enough to support the structure.

The easiest way to supply drainage is to slope the ground away from your structure so water will run off naturally. If the ground does not slope naturally, dig a drainage channel or channels to carry water away. Notice where water runoff flows naturally and install trenches there.

If runoff is light, dig trenches about 1 foot deep and line with 1 to 2 inches of gravel. If possible, direct the runoff downhill into irrigation wells for trees and shrubs. This form of water harvesting has dual benefits: it takes care of excess water and it supplies plants with needed moisture.

If runoff is heavy, further engineering will be

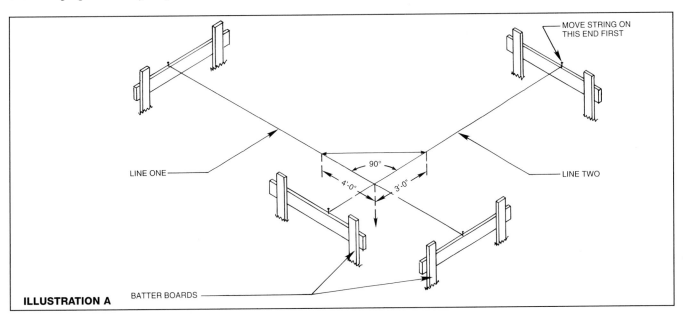

ILLUSTRATION A

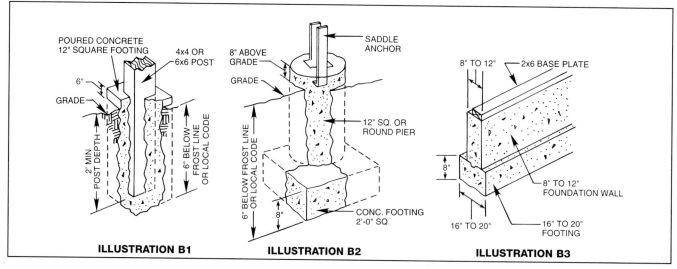

ILLUSTRATION B1   ILLUSTRATION B2   ILLUSTRATION B3

required, such as laying perforated pipe, or lining the trenches with concrete. Consult with an architect or engineer to see if these or additional methods are required to handle heavy runoff.

Remove weeds and turf: Getting weeds out of the way before you begin to build makes construction easier. Hoe or pull out weeds in small areas. In larger areas, a small cultivator can be used to turn over the soil. Keep cultivation shallow or weed seeds will be brought up to the soil surface to germinate.

To prevent future weed growth, lay down heavy black plastic sheeting (at least 6 mils thick). Newly available "fabric mulch" is also good for this purpose. It prevents weed growth, yet allows water to pass through and soak into the soil, which results in less runoff downgrade. Cover the sheeting or mulch with about 2 inches of pea gravel to hold it in place.

PROJECT LAYOUT

A simple surveying procedure allows you to be sure your project will be built square, with true 90-degree angles. Batter boards are used to square the starting corner of your project. This corner could be the outside wall of the foundation or the center point of your first post. The first step is to construct a right triangle using the "3-4-5 Method" described below. (Actually, any multiple of 3-4-5, such as 6-8-10, or 12-16-20 will work—the larger the better.)

The 3-4-5 Method

Using stakes and string, run a line (Line One) parallel to what you have determined will be the front of your project. Install batter boards as shown in *Illustration A* (see page 5) and attach string. Be sure the batter boards are far enough apart to build your project between. Install a second set of batter boards perpendicular to Line One and attach Line Two. Using a length of string or a measuring tape, measure 4 feet along Line One from the point where it intersects Line Two. Mark that point with a piece of string that will

slide. Measure 3 feet along Line Two from the Line One/Line Two intersection point and mark it with a piece of string that will slide. Next, measure 3 feet along Line Two from the Line One/Line Two intersection and mark it in the same manner. Now, measure the distance across from the string you tied to Line One to the string on Line Two. The corner is exactly square when this distance is five feet.

Adjust the string on the far end of Line Two and slide the string on Line One until the measurements equal the correct ratio. Double-check the accuracy by placing a carpenter's square in the corner. This process will establish a point with a perfect 90-degree angle from which to begin building your project. Regardless of where the point is it will become the main reference point for the entire project.

FOUNDATIONS, FOOTINGS AND PIERS

A poor foundation can ruin even the best project. *Illustration B* presents three options for a foundation, using piers and a poured concrete wall on a footer. Other methods include a concrete block foundation wall, or even placing your structure directly on pre-cast concrete piers.

Local codes vary in requirements for footing sizes and depths. If you are in an area where the ground freezes, footings must be placed at the code-recommended depth below the soil level. *Be sure to check the codes in your area before installing the footings for your project.*

Be sure to check the codes in your area before installing the footings for your project.

Piers, footings and foundations are the base of any project. Piers are formed from concrete, either pre-cast or "pour-your-own." To pour your own, either build

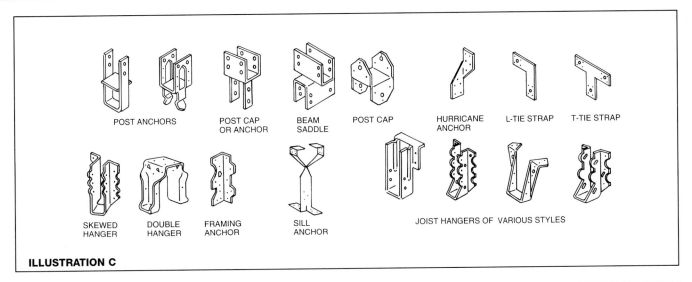

POST ANCHORS   POST CAP OR ANCHOR   BEAM SADDLE   POST CAP   HURRICANE ANCHOR   L-TIE STRAP   T-TIE STRAP

SKEWED HANGER   DOUBLE HANGER   FRAMING ANCHOR   SILL ANCHOR   JOIST HANGERS OF VARIOUS STYLES

ILLUSTRATION C

your own forms from lumber, or use the ready-made forms of wax-impregnated cardboard, available in cylinder or block shapes, at local home-improvement or lumber supply stores.

Foundation walls are commonly made by pouring the footer in a ditch to the required depth (8" to 12"), and then building forms. The foundation wall is poured on top of the footing. An optional method is to set a block foundation wall on top of the footing. Pre-cast piers are available in various sizes and with drift-pin connections. These can be set on grade or sunken into the ground, depending on the type you select.

ATTACH PROJECT TO FOUNDATION

Whether your project is sitting on posts or a foundation wall, all wood within 12 inches of the soil should be treated as required by most codes. *Illustrations B1 and B2* show the two most common ways to attach a post to a footing or pier. By setting metal connectors in poured concrete you will create a strong connection less susceptible to wood rot than simply sinking a post in concrete. All connectors should be of the highest quality 16- to 18-gauge hot-dipped galvanized steel. Ensure that all nails, bolts, nuts and other fittings exposed to the elements are also of galvanized steel.

Illustration B3 shows the base plate on the top of the foundation wall secured with anchor bolts. This plate will support the floor joist.

Many additional foundation options are available, such as slab flooring with anchor ties, block walls and others. The one you need will be indicated in the detailed set of plans for each project.

Leveling Post Height

If you are pouring a foundation wall or laying block, the top should be perfectly level for placing the sill plate. Since posts set in or on top of a footing or pier may vary in height, follow these guidelines. Use a post 6 inches longer than needed to allow for variations. After the concrete has set, string a level line to find the top of the

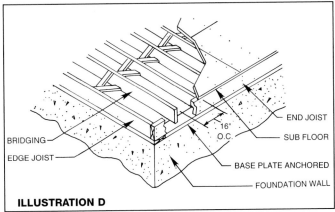

BRIDGING
EDGE JOIST
END JOIST
16" O.C.
SUB FLOOR
BASE PLATE ANCHORED
FOUNDATION WALL

ILLUSTRATION D

post height needed for your project. Level the posts and cut to the same height prior to attaching floor joists or beams.

Making Framing Connections

Joists, rafters and even sill plate connections can be made stronger by using manufactured metal framing devices. *Illustration C* shows a variety of connectors and their applications. Other connectors are available which are easy to install and provide a strong connection.

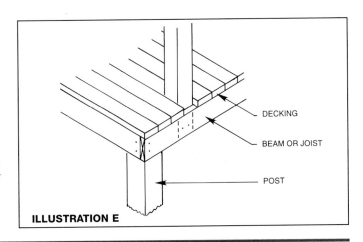

DECKING
BEAM OR JOIST
POST

ILLUSTRATION E

STANDARD FLOOR CONSTRUCTION

Of all possible structural systems, platform framing is the easiest and most common method used. The entire floor frame is constructed first, including the subflooring, as in *Illustration D*. In this way, the floor surface serves as a platform for the structure's walls. If a slab is poured, it then acts as the platform.

To construct a floor frame, a sill plate is attached to the foundation wall with anchor bolts. Then the header joists and edge joists are set upright and nailed to the sill plate. Header, edge and regular joists are all constructed using the same size lumber. The sill plate will usually be a 2x6. Floor joists are normally placed 16 inches on center with splices only occurring above a beam. The subflooring extends to the edges of the floor framing structure.

If you are building a gazebo or other structure using 5x4 or 5x2 decking, the joists may attach to the posts or beams with the decking extended to the edge. It may also be modified for railings or columns, as shown in *Illustration E*.

Structural Bracing

Additional bracing can be provided with blocking or cross-bridging. "Blocking" uses boards the same dimension as the joists, placed between the joists for added support. "Cross-bridging" uses 2x3s or 2x4s placed in an X pattern between joists for added support. If blocking boards are cut precisely to size before joists are installed, they can serve as a measure to ensure correct spacing between joists. Stagger the blocking pattern to make it easier to install.

Be sure all joists are installed at the same level. Because the actual project flooring goes on top of the joists, they must be the same height or the surface of the

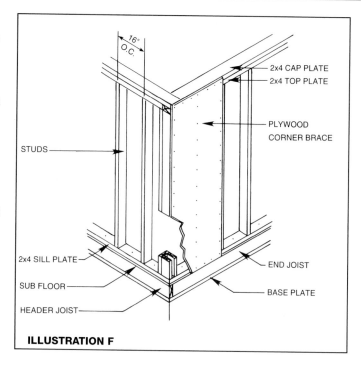

ILLUSTRATION F

- 2x4 CAP PLATE
- 2x4 TOP PLATE
- PLYWOOD CORNER BRACE
- STUDS
- 2x4 SILL PLATE
- SUB FLOOR
- HEADER JOIST
- END JOIST
- BASE PLATE
- 16" O.C.

floor will be uneven. To check, place a line over the joists and pull it tight. It will be easy to tell which joists are too high or too low and need to be adjusted.

Splicing Joists

Joists, like beams, must be spliced when they do not span the entire distance between beams. Splice only above a beam to ensure needed support. Use a wood or metal cleat, or overlap the joist at the beam. Extend the joint 8 or more inches beyond the sides of each beam to increase the strength of the junction and to allow room for the splice.

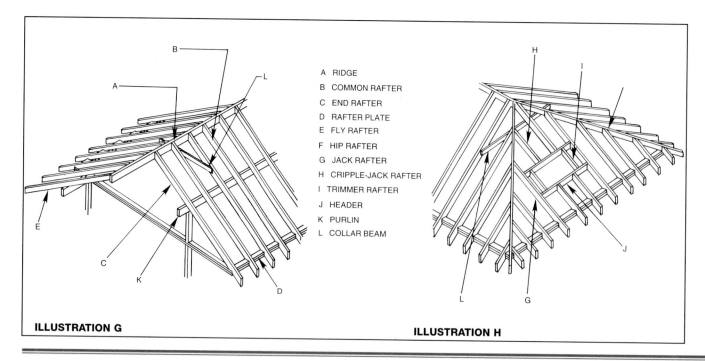

A RIDGE
B COMMON RAFTER
C END RAFTER
D RAFTER PLATE
E FLY RAFTER
F HIP RAFTER
G JACK RAFTER
H CRIPPLE-JACK RAFTER
I TRIMMER RAFTER
J HEADER
K PURLIN
L COLLAR BEAM

ILLUSTRATION G

ILLUSTRATION H

If the joist spans over 8 feet, apply a cross-brace or blocking to prevent twisting. The longer the distance, the more likely the joist is to twist. If the floor span of your project is 8 feet or less, the end headers normally provide enough support so that cross-bracing is not required. Use blocking for added support for joists that are 2x4, 2x6, or 2x8, but for joists that are 2x10 or larger, install wood or metal cross bracing.

STANDARD WALL CONSTRUCTION

In platform framing, exterior walls and interior partitions have a single 2x4-plate (2x6 when studs are 2x6s) that rests on the subfloor. This is called the bottom or sole plate. The top of the walls have a doubled plate called the top plate, or cap plate, that supports ceiling joists, and, in most cases, roof rafters. The walls of a structure usually are built lying flat on the subfloor, then raised into position in one section. Wall studs are also normally placed 16" on center, but if 2x6 studs are used, then 24" on center may be acceptable.

There are a number of ways to construct the corner post. The method shown in *Illustration F* is one of the most common. Also shown is a sheet of exterior plywood at the corner. This is used as corner bracing. There are other methods, such as a 2x4 notched at a 45-degree angle, or metal "X" bracing, but using plywood is the easiest and fastest method. For small structures with ⅝" T-111 siding, or equal, this could also serve as the needed corner bracing and is sufficient for most codes.

Prior to starting the wall construction, be sure to verify all rough opening sizes for doors, windows, etc. All headers above the doors and windows are constructed of 2x material, which is really 1½" thick. With 2 2x6s or 2x8s with a ½" plywood spacer, you can build a header to support almost any window or door span for the projects in this book.

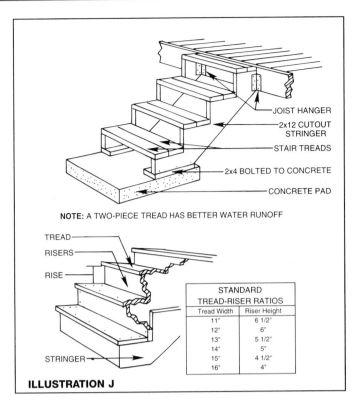

NOTE: A TWO-PIECE TREAD HAS BETTER WATER RUNOFF

STANDARD TREAD-RISER RATIOS	
Tread Width	Riser Height
11"	6 1/2"
12"	6"
13"	5 1/2"
14"	5"
15"	4 1/2"
16"	4"

ILLUSTRATION J

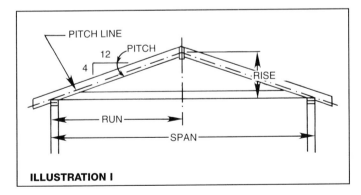

ILLUSTRATION I

ROOF FRAMING

Up to the cap plate or top plate, the method of construction depends on the type of framing system used. *Above* the cap plate, the method of construction depends mainly on the style of the roof indicated for the structure.

Two structures built from identical plans can look considerably different when only the style of the roof is changed. The two most common roof styles are the gable (*Illustration G*) and the hip (*Illustration H*). For garden amenities structures, other styles are also used, such as a shed roof or gambrel roof, plus variations and combinations of each style.

There are five roof-framing terms you should know, which are used in calculating rafter length: span, rise, run, pitch, and pitch line, as shown in *Illustration I*. To construct a roof you will need to use a rafter square, available from local suppliers. Get either a metal angle or a triangular square. The least expensive model is a plastic triangular square. It comes with instructions on how to use it to measure rafters, cut angles, and cut "the bird's mouth," which is the part that sits on the wall cap plate. Because cutting the roof rafters is probably the most difficult task involved in building a garden structure, the rafter square is the most useful tool you can have.

STAIRS AND STEPS

Most outdoor projects require stairs and steps to provide exits to ground level. Stairs are composed of the *tread,* the surface you walk on, and the *riser,* the vertical distance between steps. Stairs are usually 4-, 5-, or 6-feet wide. It is important that you retain a constant *riser-to-tread* ratio. This ensures an equal distance between steps to avoid missteps and stumbles. A common riser-to-tread ratio is 6:12, which can be built by using two 2x6 treads and a 2x6 riser. For example, if the width of the tread is 12 inches, the next step should "rise" 6 inches.

The supports to which the steps are attached are called *stair stringers* or *carriage*, usually built from a 2x12. Steps can also be constructed as a single step from floor to ground, or from one floor level to another. Some steps are constructed as a separate level, a kind of continuous step, from one floor level to another. *Illustration J* shows the options for stringers and treads, plus a chart indicating standard tread-riser ratios.

INSULATION

If you are going to heat or cool your structure, you may want to insulate the walls and ceiling. If so, the normal wall insulation is R-19 in cold climates, with R-38 for the ceiling. R-values vary according to climate, so check with your local supplier for the requirements in your area.

GLOSSARY

Anchor bolt: A device for connecting wood members to concrete or masonry.

Blocking: Used for added support for floor joists and to prevent twisting.

Balustrade: A complete handrail assembly. Includes rails, balusters, subrails and fillets.

Batter board: Simple wooden forms used early in construction to mark the corners of the structure and the height of foundation walls.

Beam: A horizontal framing member of wood or steel, no less than 5 inches thick and at least 2 inches wider than it is thick.

Board: Any piece of lumber more than 1 inch wide, but less than 2 inches wider in thickness.

Common rafter: Any of several identical structural members of a roof that run at right angles to walls and end at right angles to main roof framing members.

Concrete: A mixture of cement, sand, gravel and water.

Cross-bridging: Diagonal wood braces that form an "X" between floor joists.

Drip edge: A strip of metal used to protect the edges of a roof structure from water damage.

Drywall: A method of covering wall and ceiling surfaces with dry materials, rather than wet materials such as plaster. Refers primarily to the application of gypsum wallboard, also called drywall.

Edge joist: The outer joist of a floor or ceiling system that runs parallel to other joists. See *header joist*.

Foundation: The part of a building that rests on a footing and supports all of the structure above it.

Frame: The wood skeleton of a building. Also called framing.

Header: Any structural wood member used across the ends of an opening to support the cut ends of shortened framing members in a floor, wall or roof.

Header joist: The outer joist of a floor or ceiling system that runs across other joists. See *edge joist*.

Joist: A horizontal structural member that, together with other similar members, supports a floor or ceiling system.

O.C.: Abbreviation for On Centers, a measurement from one center line to the next, usually of structural members.

Ridgeboard: The horizontal board at the ridge to which the top ends of rafters are attached. Also called a "ridge beam" or "ridge pole."

Plans You Can Build

For Yard & Garden Structures

Building a beautiful or practical outdoor addition in your yard or garden should be like adding icing to a cake. A something-extra, value-added, just-for-fun project from concept through completion. Whether you built your home or had it built—just moved in or have been there for years—take a look around with a "wish list" in mind. Given your lifestyle, what would you and your family use most? A garden swing? A romantic gazebo? A potting shed? Or a just-what-you've-always-wanted shed for tools?

On the following pages are illustrations for 42 projects, some practical, some whimsical, but all designed to enhance your lifestyle and make creative use of your outdoor areas. Complete construction blueprints are available for you to order for each project. (The Compost Bin, on page 44, has complete instructions right in the book!) All are ready for you to build or have a professional contractor build for you.

Each is easily adaptable to almost any style or type of home or outdoor area.

Blueprint packages include everything you will need to complete these projects—frontal sheet, materials list, floor plan, framing plan, and where needed, elevations. In addition, Home Planners offers a Gazebo Construction Details package which provides additional information for building gazebos, as well as a Standard Construction Details package which gives advice on basic building techniques. (See page 92 for more information.)

Take your time as you look through the following pages. Imagine how each project shown would look in your yard or garden, and the enjoyment and/or convenience your family would receive. When you have decided on the project, simply turn to page 92 for order information. We'll rush the plans to you and answer any questions you have.

The Ornament
PLAN G246

Features at a Glance:

✦ Outstanding Focal Point
✦ Easy to Build
✦ Large Floor Area

PLAN G246. *SEE PAGE 92 TO ORDER COMPLETE
CONSTRUCTION DRAWINGS FOR THIS PLAN.*

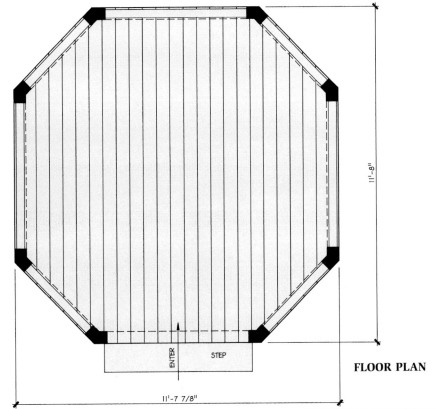

11'-8"

11'-7 7/8"

ENTER   STEP

FLOOR PLAN

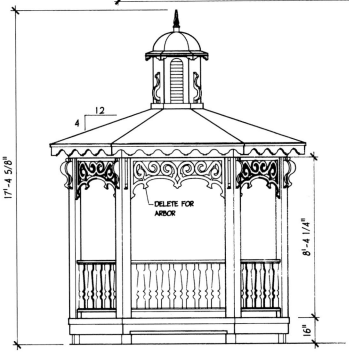

12

4

17'-4 5/8"

DELETE FOR ARBOR

8'-4 1/4"

16"

FRONT ELEVATION

*R*eflecting the image "gingerbread" is intended to convey, the delightful gazebo shown on the cover will be the focal point of your landscape . . . the icing on the cake . . . the star atop the Holiday tree! The floor area of nearly 144 square feet is large enough for a table and 4 to 6 chairs. Or, add built-in benches to increase the seating capacity to accommodate 20 people.

Painted white with pink asphalt roof shingles, this gazebo has a cool summery appearance. Or, you can build it with unpainted, treated materials and cedar shake shingles for an entirely different effect. Either exterior design will provide an outstanding setting for years of outdoor relaxation and entertainment. The jaunty cupola complete with spire adds a stately look to this single-entrance structure. The plans also include an optional arbor, which can be incorporated into the entrance of the gazebo.

Star Struck
PLAN G218

Features at a Glance:

- ◆ Large Capacity
- ◆ Unique Appearance
- ◆ Easy to Modify

PLAN G218. *SEE PAGE 92 TO ORDER COMPLETE*
CONSTRUCTION DRAWINGS FOR THIS PLAN.

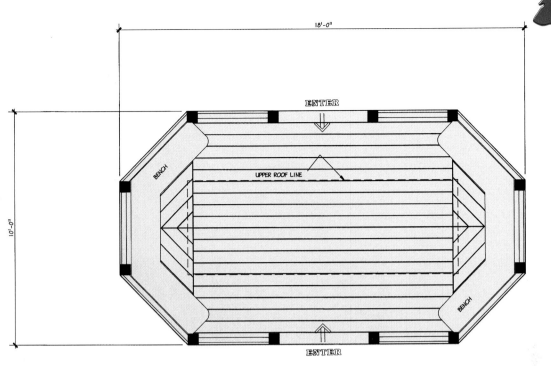

18'-0"

10'-0"

ENTER

BENCH

UPPER ROOF LINE

BENCH

ENTER

FLOOR PLAN

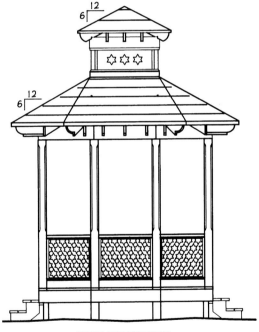

12
6⌐

12
6⌐

SIDE ELEVATION

*D*esigned for serious entertaining, the size alone—576 square feet—lets you know this gazebo is unique. The star-lattice railing design, built-in benches and raised center roof with accent trim make this structure as practical as it is attractive. Large enough for small parties, there is built-in seating for about 20 people and enough floor area for another 10 to 20. Ideal for entertaining, the addition of lights and a wet bar make this design an important extension of any home.

Roof lines and overhang can be modified to give an oriental effect, or removed completely to give a carousel-like appearance. Although this double-entrance, pass-through gazebo looks complicated, it is fairly simple to build with the right tools and materials.

Country Garden
PLAN G221

Features at a Glance:

◆ Built-in Planters
◆ Large Area
◆ Open-Air Lattice Work

PLAN G221. *SEE PAGE 92 TO ORDER COMPLETE
CONSTRUCTION DRAWINGS FOR THIS PLAN.*

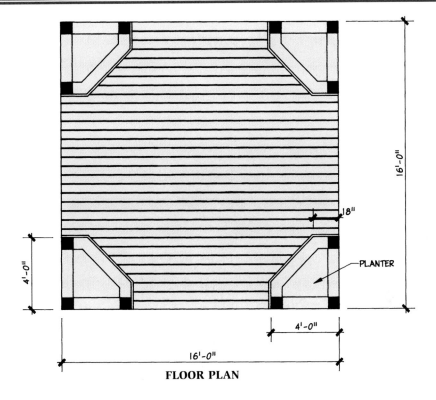

FLOOR PLAN

16'-0"

18"

PLANTER

4'-0"

4'-0"

16'-0"

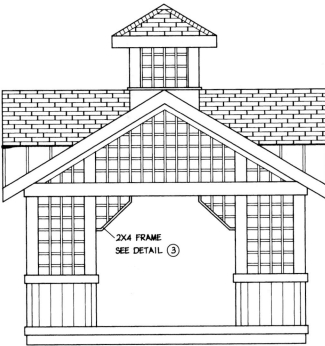

2X4 FRAME
SEE DETAIL ③

SIDE ELEVATION

The built-in planters and open roof areas of this multiple-entrance gazebo make this design a gardener's dream-come-true. The open roof allows sun and rain ample access to the planters and gives the structure a definite country-garden effect. Built with or without a cupola, the open-air lattice work in the walls and roof complements a wide variety of landscapes and home designs. A creative gardener will soon enhance this charming gazebo with a wealth of plants and vines. Tuck a bird bath or bubbling fountain into a corner to further the garden setting. The large design—256 square feet—ensures that both you and nature have plenty of room to share all that this gazebo has to offer. It easily accommodates a table and chairs when you invite your guests to this outdoor hide-a-way.

Neo-Classic Gazebo
PLAN G108

Features at a Glance:

- ✦ Classic Lines
- ✦ Spacious
- ✦ Complements Many Housing Styles

PLAN G108. *SEE PAGE 92 TO ORDER COMPLETE CONSTRUCTION DRAWINGS FOR THIS PLAN.*

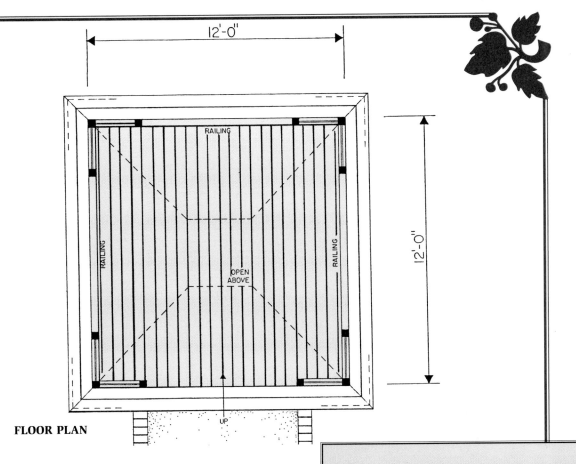

12'-0"

12'-0"

RAILING

RAILING

RAILING

OPEN
ABOVE

UP

FLOOR PLAN

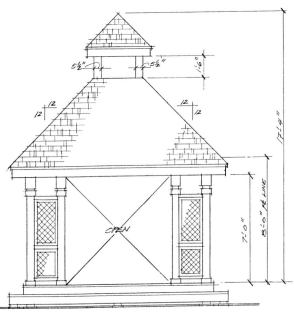

5½" 5½" 1'6"

12 12   12 12

17'-4"

8'-0" PLATE LINE

7'-0"

OPEN

FRONT ELEVATION

*B*est suited for larger lots—at least a half acre—this gazebo provides a prime spot for entertaining. At 200-plus square feet of decking, it has as much surface space as the average family room. And, topping out at just under 17½', it's as tall as a one-story house!

Boasting many neo-classic features—perfect proportions, columns, bases—it blends well with a variety of housing styles: Cape, Georgian, Farmhouse and others. The cupola is an added touch that lets light flow to the decking below. Cedar or redwood would be a good choice for building materials.

American Bandstand
PLAN G217

Features at a Glance:

◆ Easy Square Shape
◆ Large Floor Area
◆ Accommodates Crawl Space

PLAN G217. *SEE PAGE 92 TO ORDER COMPLETE
CONSTRUCTION DRAWINGS FOR THIS PLAN.*

16'-0"

22'-4"

UP

UP

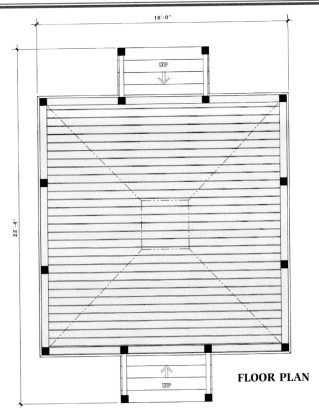

FLOOR PLAN

SIDE ELEVATION

Dance the night away in this double-entrance, pass-through style gazebo. By day, the open-air construction provides a clear view in all directions. The large floor area of 256 square feet seats 12 to 16 people comfortably or nicely accommodates musicians or entertainers for a lawn party. The decorative cupola can be lowered, louvered, or removed to create just the appearance you want. Or, add an antique weather vane just for fun.

This gazebo has five steps up which gives it a large crawl space for access to any utilities which are added. Its square shape allows for simple cutting and floor framing, plus easy assembly of the roof frame. The trim and hand rails are simple to construct or modify to achieve several different design effects.

Gazebos

Trellis-Go-Round
PLAN G220

Features at a Glance:

- ✦ Trellis Roof
- ✦ Simple to Construct
- ✦ Garden Options

PLAN G220. *SEE PAGE 92 TO ORDER COMPLETE CONSTRUCTION DRAWINGS FOR THIS PLAN.*

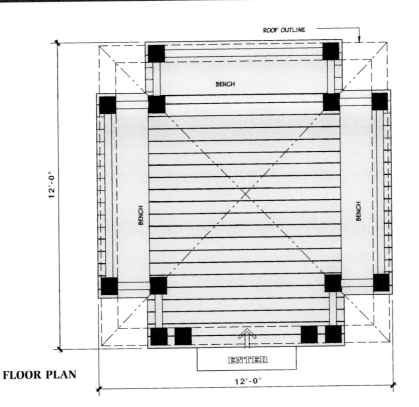

ROOF OUTLINE

BENCH

BENCH

BENCH

12'-0"

12'-0"

ENTER

FLOOR PLAN

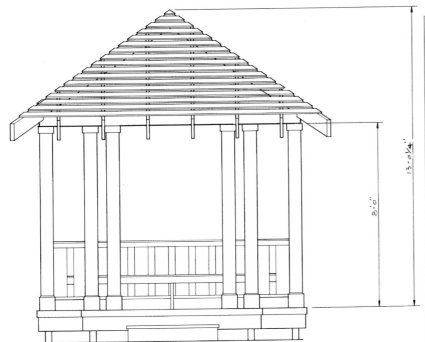

13'-0¾"

8'-0"

FRONT ELEVATION

*U*p, down and green all around! Light and airy, the unique trellis roof of this innovative single-entrance gazebo is just waiting for your favorite perennial vines. To extend the green-all-around look, modify the railings to a lattice pattern and train vines or grapes—or roses, for a splash of color—to experience nature all around you. The inset corners of the design provide plenty of space for planting. Simple lines make this delightful gazebo easy to construct, with no cumbersome cutting or gingerbread. The large area—100 square feet—provides built-in seating for 9 people. This flexible design could be modified to a closed roof with any standard roof sheathing and shingles, and the single entrance design can be altered to accommodate multiple entrances.

Kaleidoscope
PLAN G219

Features at a Glance:

✦ Operable Louvers
✦ Masonry Base
✦ Optional Copper Cover

PLAN G219. *SEE PAGE 92 TO ORDER COMPLETE CONSTRUCTION DRAWINGS FOR THIS PLAN.*

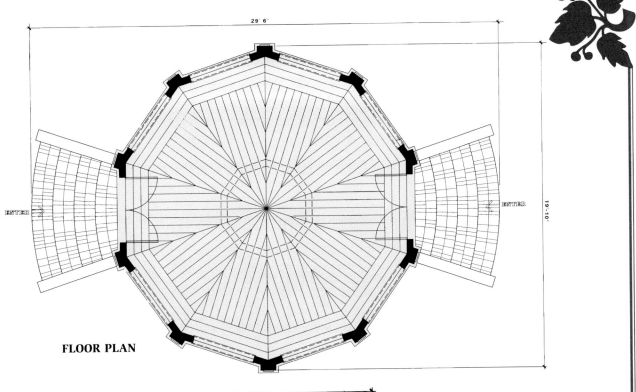

FLOOR PLAN

29' 6"

19' - 10"

ENTER

ENTER

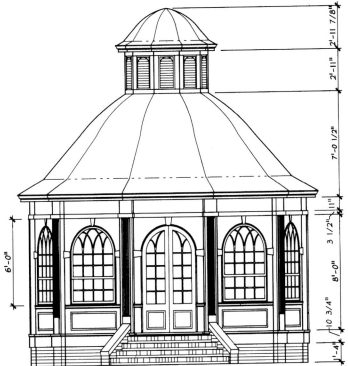

FRONT ELEVATION

2'-11 7/8"

2'-11"

7'-0 1/2"

11"

3 1/2"

8'-0"

10 3/4"

1'-4"

6'-0"

*S*hining copper on the cupola and shimmering glass windows all around enhance this double-entrance gazebo with dancing light and color. The many windows allow natural light to engulf the interior, making it a perfect studio. Easy to heat and cool, this gazebo contains operable louvers in the cupola to increase the flow of air. An exhaust fan could be added to the cupola to further maximize air flow.

The masonry base with brick steps gives the structure a definite feeling of both elegance and permanence. The roof structure is made from standard framing materials with the cupola adorned with a copper cover. If cost is a factor, the cupola roof could be made of asphalt shingles and the glass windows could be eliminated.

American Colonial
PLAN G216

Features at a Glance:

- ✦ Solid Base
- ✦ Vented Crawl Space
- ✦ Benches for Increased Seating

PLAN G216. *SEE PAGE 92 TO ORDER COMPLETE CONSTRUCTION DRAWINGS FOR THIS PLAN.*

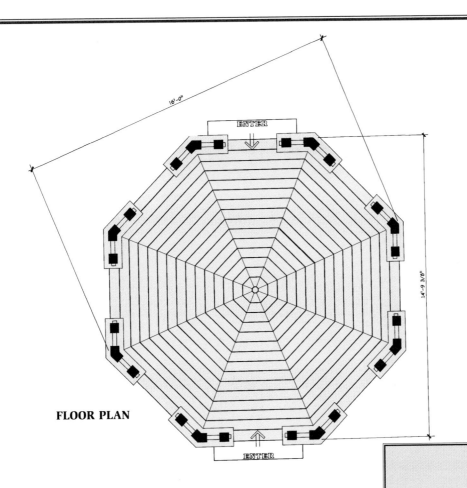

FLOOR PLAN

16'-0"

14'-9 3/8"

ENTER

ENTER

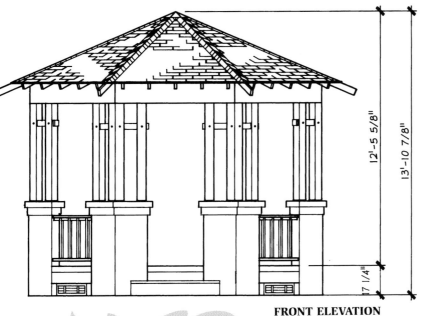

FRONT ELEVATION

12'-5 5/8"

13'-10 7/8"

17 1/4"

With a solidly built base and heavy braced columns, this gazebo will stand the test of time. Add electricity and water to make a perfect garden spot for entertaining. This design features an accented roof overhang and open soffit. The base could be stuccoed for a "Tudor" effect.

This two-step-up structure has a vented crawl space in the base to give quick access to any utilities which might be added. The floor area is approximately 160 square feet and will accommodate 8 to 10 people in standard chairs. The double entrance can be modified to a single entrance, with benches added to increase seating to twenty-one.

American Classic
PLAN G215

Features at a Glance:

♦ Adapts to a Variety of Styles
♦ Large Floor Area
♦ Basic Design

PLAN G215. *SEE PAGE 92 TO ORDER COMPLETE CONSTRUCTION DRAWINGS FOR THIS PLAN.*

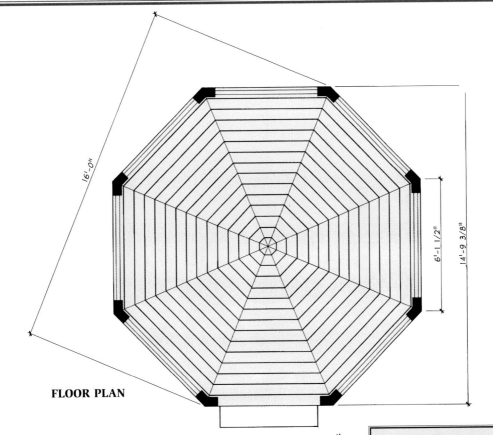

FLOOR PLAN

16'-0"

6'-1 1/2"

14'-9 3/8"

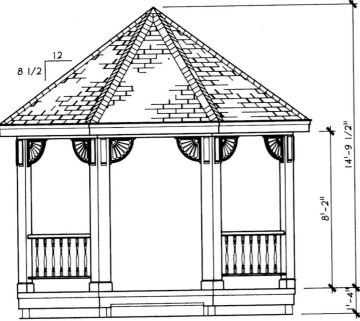

12

8 1/2

14'-9 1/2"

8'-2"

1'-4"

FRONT ELEVATION

*T*his all-American single-entrance gazebo is simple to construct and easy to adapt to a variety of styles. All materials are available in most areas with no special cutting for trim or rails. This gazebo is distinguished by its simple design and large floor area. The traditional eight-sided configuration and overall area of approximately 160 square feet allow for the placement of furniture with ample seating for 8 to 10 people.

Build as shown, or modify the trim and railings to give a totally different appearance. If multiple entrance/exit access is desired, simply eliminate the rails as needed. Access to the ground is a single step which could be easily modified for a low ramp.

Stylish Storage
PLAN G107

Features at a Glance:

- ✦ Flexible Design
- ✦ Complements Many House Styles
- ✦ Creates Additional Outdoor Living Area

PLAN G107. *SEE PAGE 92 TO ORDER COMPLETE CONSTRUCTION DRAWINGS FOR THIS PLAN.*

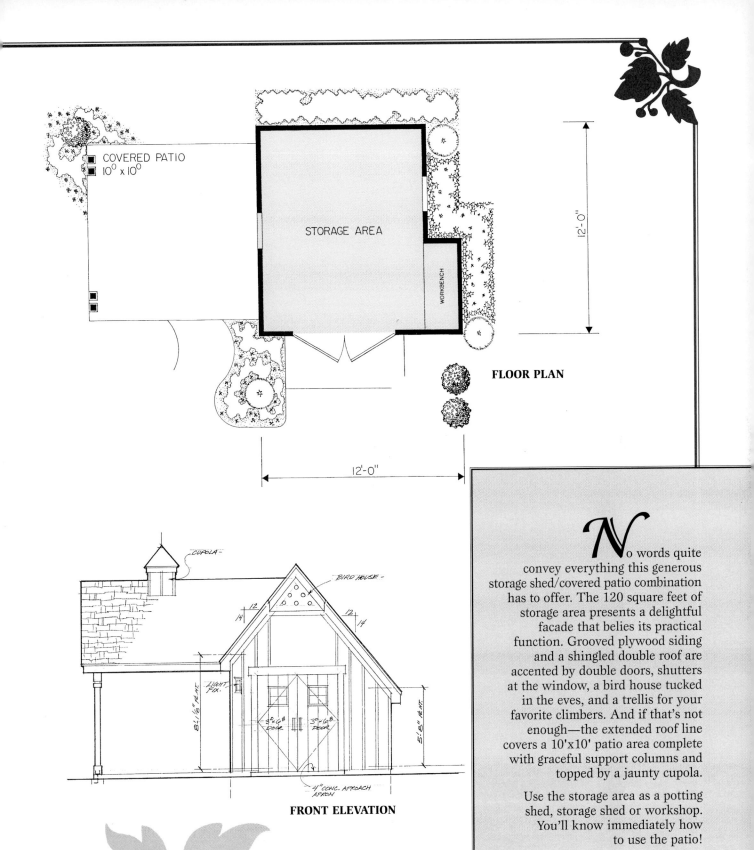

COVERED PATIO
10⁰ x 10⁰

STORAGE AREA

WORKBENCH

12'-0"

FLOOR PLAN

12'-0"

CUPOLA

BIRD HOUSE

12
14
12
14

LIGHT FIX.

8'-1½" FL. HT.

3⁹x6⁸ DOOR
3⁹x6⁸ DOOR

5'-8" FL. HT.

4" CONC. APROACH APRON

FRONT ELEVATION

$\mathcal{N}$o words quite convey everything this generous storage shed/covered patio combination has to offer. The 120 square feet of storage area presents a delightful facade that belies its practical function. Grooved plywood siding and a shingled double roof are accented by double doors, shutters at the window, a bird house tucked in the eves, and a trellis for your favorite climbers. And if that's not enough—the extended roof line covers a 10'x10' patio area complete with graceful support columns and topped by a jaunty cupola.

Use the storage area as a potting shed, storage shed or workshop. You'll know immediately how to use the patio!

Little House in the Garden
PLAN G247

Features at a Glance:

- ✦ Easy to Build
- ✦ Functional
- ✦ Multi-Use

PLAN G247. *SEE PAGE 92 TO ORDER COMPLETE CONSTRUCTION DRAWINGS FOR THIS PLAN.*

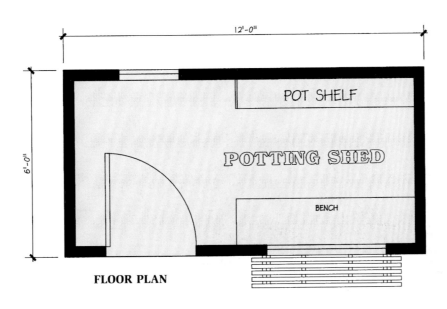

FLOOR PLAN

12'-0"

6'-0"

POT SHELF

POTTING SHED

BENCH

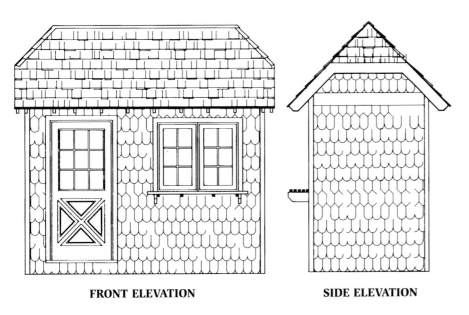

FRONT ELEVATION   **SIDE ELEVATION**

*D*esigned to accent its surroundings, this cozy little building keeps all your garden tools and supplies at your fingertips. It is shown on the back cover with cedar shake shingles on the roof and cedar siding. You can vary the materials to create the appearance best suited to your site. This 5'x4' structure is large enough to accommodate a potting bench, shelves and an area for garden tools. The window above the potting bench allows ample light, but electricity could be added easily.

Designed to be built on a concrete slab, you could use treated lumber for the floor joists, and sit it right on the ground. To convert this shed design to a playhouse, simply change the window shelf into a planter and add a step with a handrail at the door.

Double Duty
PLAN G222

Features at a Glance:

- ✦ Dual Functions
- ✦ Skylight
- ✦ Large Storage Capacity

PLAN G222. *SEE PAGE 92 TO ORDER COMPLETE CONSTRUCTION DRAWINGS FOR THIS PLAN.*

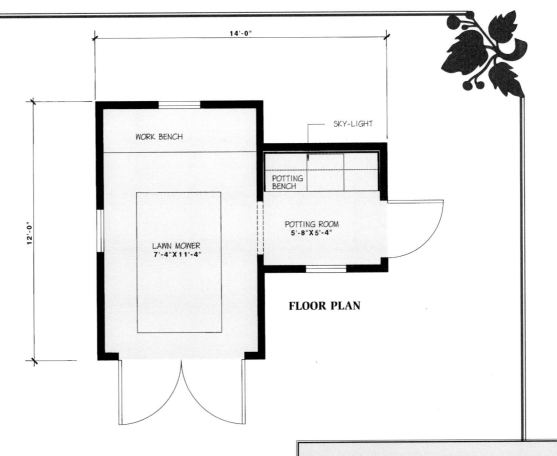

14'-0"

12'-0"

WORK BENCH

SKY-LIGHT

POTTING
BENCH

POTTING ROOM
5'-8" X 5'-4"

LAWN MOWER
7'-4" X 11'-4"

FLOOR PLAN

5/4
TRIM

1 X 8 PRIMED HARDBOARD SIDING
6" TO WEATHER

FRONT ELEVATION

*O*pen the double doors of this multi-purpose structure and it's a mini-garage for tools. Enter by the single door, and it's a potting shed complete with potting bench and skylight. The tool shed section is large enough—8'x12'—to house the largest lawn tractor, with room to spare for other garden equipment such as shovels, rakes, lawn trimmers and hoses.

With windows on all sides and a skylight above the potting bench, the interior has plenty of natural light, although the addition of electrical wiring would make this structure even more practical. The design is shown in a Victorian style, but a different appearance can be accomplished by modifying the trim, windows and siding to match any gable-roof home design.

"Boat"anical Beauty
PLAN G223

Features at a Glance:

- ◆ Roomy Studio/Loft
- ◆ Ample Storage Area
- ◆ Lots of Natural Light

PLAN G223. *SEE PAGE 92 TO ORDER COMPLETE CONSTRUCTION DRAWINGS FOR THIS PLAN.*

Lawn Sheds

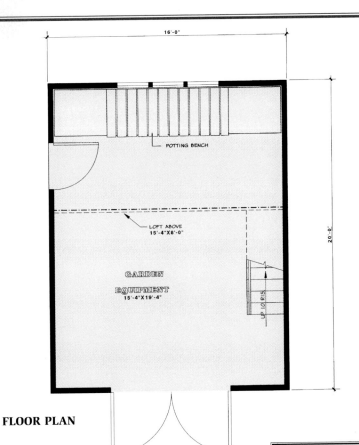

16'-0"

20'-0"

POTTING BENCH

LOFT ABOVE
15'-4"X8'-0"

GARDEN
EQUIPMENT
15'-4"X19'-4"

UP 10 RIS

FLOOR PLAN

FRONT ELEVATION

*T*his large multi-level garden shed can be easily modified to become a boat house if yours is a nautical family. It encompasses a generous 320 square feet, plus a convenient storage loft, and is totally contemporary in design. As a lawn or garden shed, there is ample room for all your garden equipment, with a separate area for potting plants. The built-in potting bench features removable planks to accommodate flats of flowers in various sizes. The roomy loft provides 133 square feet of safe storage area for chemicals, fertilizers or other lawn-care products.

Natural light floods the interior through multiple windows in the rear wall and in the front, across from the storage loft. This practical structure can also be used as a studio or, placed at the water's edge, it can be easily converted to a boat house by adding 4'x4' columns used as piers in lieu of the slab floor.

Rural Hideaway
PLAN G226

Features at a Glance:

- ✦ Large Overall Area
- ✦ Roomy Loft
- ✦ Separate Work Area

PLAN G226. *SEE PAGE 92 TO ORDER COMPLETE CONSTRUCTION DRAWINGS FOR THIS PLAN.*

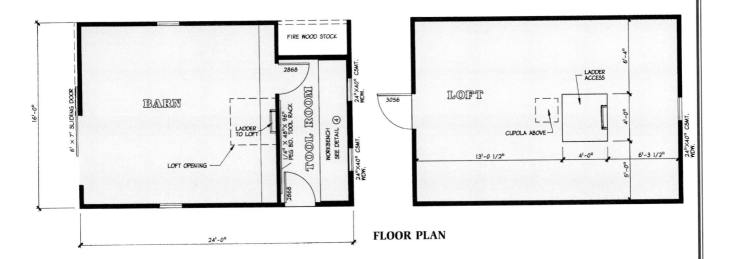

FLOOR PLAN

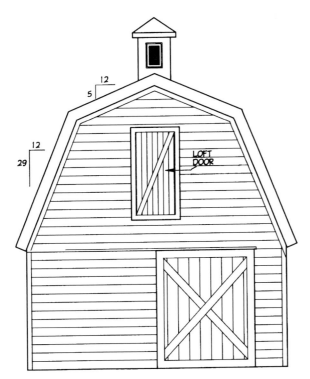

FRONT ELEVATION

*T*his large, sturdy lawn shed is not quite "as big as a barn," but almost! A combined area of 768 square feet includes a 24'x16' loft area with access by ladder or stairway. The structure is built entirely of standard framing materials requiring no special beams or cutting.

An ideal hideaway for the serious artist, this structure could serve a myriad of other uses including a second garage, a game house, or even as a barn for small livestock. Or, expand the design to include utilities and a bathroom to provide a secluded guest room.

The large tool room at the back has a built-in work bench with plenty of natural light, plus entrances from inside or outside. If your house has a fireplace, space is provided for a built-in wood stockpile area. The same space could be used to extend the length of the tool room. A 6'x7' sliding-door entrance with crossbars, and a louvered cupola, accent the rural effect.

Lawn Sheds

Two-Door Tudor
PLAN G225

Features at a Glance:

- ✦ Charming Window Seat
- ✦ Separate Storage Room
- ✦ Large Floor Area

PLAN G225. *SEE PAGE 92 TO ORDER COMPLETE CONSTRUCTION DRAWINGS FOR THIS PLAN.*

Lawn Sheds

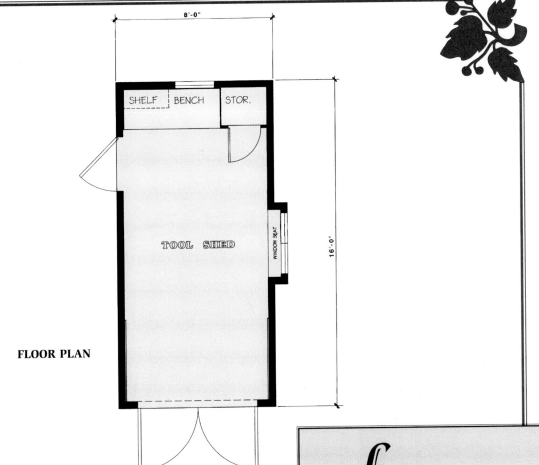

8'-0"

SHELF | BENCH | STOR.

TOOL SHED

16'-0"

WINDOW SEAT

FLOOR PLAN

1X6 TRIM

SIDE ELEVATION

*L*awn-shed extraordinaire, this appealing design can be easily converted from the Tudor style shown here, to match just about any exterior design you prefer. In addition to serving as a lawn shed, this versatile structure also can be used as a craft studio, a pool house, or a delightful playhouse for your children.

The double doors and large floor area provide ample access and storage capacity for lawn tractors and other large pieces of equipment. A handy built-in work bench offers needed space for potting plants or working on craft projects. A separate storage room for craft supplies, lawn-care products or pool chemicals can be locked for safety. Strategically placed on your site, this charming building could be designed to be a reflection of your home in miniature.

The Convertible
PLAN G224

Features at a Glance:

✦ Versatile Design
✦ Moveable
✦ Ample Storage

PLAN G224. *SEE PAGE 92 TO ORDER COMPLETE CONSTRUCTION DRAWINGS FOR THIS PLAN.*

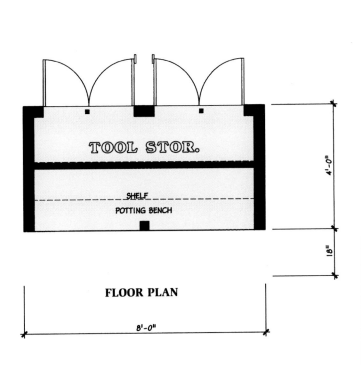

FLOOR PLAN

8'-0"

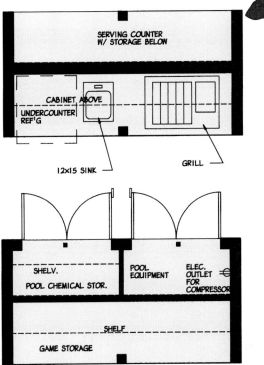

SERVING COUNTER
W/ STORAGE BELOW

CABINET ABOVE

UNDERCOUNTER
REF'G

12x15 SINK

GRILL

SHELV.
POOL CHEMICAL STOR.

POOL
EQUIPMENT

ELEC.
OUTLET
FOR
COMPRESSOR

SHELF

GAME STORAGE

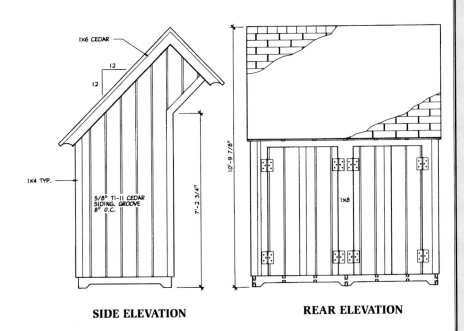

1x6 CEDAR

12

12

1x4 TYP.

5/8" T1-11 CEDAR
SIDING, GROOVE
8" O.C.

7'-2 3/4"

SIDE ELEVATION

10'-9 7/8"

1x8

REAR ELEVATION

*H*ere's a unique design that can be converted to serve a variety of functions: a tool shed, a barbecue stand, a pool-supply depot or a sports-equipment locker. Apply a little "what-if" imagination to come up with additional ways to use this versatile design to enhance your outdoor living space.

As a tool shed, this design features a large potting bench with storage above and below. Second, as a summer kitchen, it includes a built-in grill, a sink and a refrigerator. Third, for use as a pool-supply depot or equipment storage, it comes with a locker to store chemicals or valuable sports equipment safely.

This structure is designed to be moveable, but, depending on its function, could be placed on a concrete slab.

Three-Bin Composter
PLAN G248

FRANK FRETZ

Efficient recycling of biodegradable kitchen scraps and garden trimmings into useful chemical-free fertilizer has never been easier with this state-of-the-art compost bin. Simply collect and toss appropriate organic materials through the hatch of the "holding" section of this three-bin unit. The covered bin helps keep the compost moist while keeping out excess moisture. With the right amount of moisture and sufficient oxygen regulated in this well-designed unit, organic matter will heat quickly and decompose thoroughly. Then transfer and "turn" the compost between the two additional side-by-side bins for continuous composting.

Resting on a sturdy base and floor, each bin holds 27 cubic feet of organic material. Removable front slats allow you to remove a few at a time—to work with an existing pile—or all at once to transfer layers for processing from one bin to the next. *Complete instructions for this useful, easy-to-build composter follow.*

PROCEDURE FOR COMPOST BINS

Base: Nail a header to each end of the center floor joist using 16d nails. Nail the outside joists, front and back, across the ends of the headers. Nail the brace blocks in place between the joists. Locate and nail the four short floorboards across the joists where the partitions will be located, using 8d nails, as shown.

Partitions: For each of the four partitions (two outside and two inside), nail six partition boards to connect two corner posts. Nail the inside door tracks to the partition boards, 1 inch back from the front corner posts.

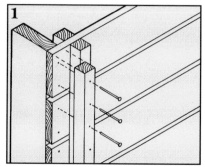

Nail the outside door tracks flush with the front of the two interior partitions. Position the assembled partitions—one on each end of the base and one on each side of the interior compartment; drill and bolt the corner posts to the outside joists.

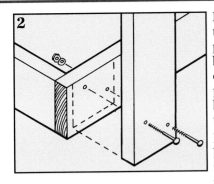

2

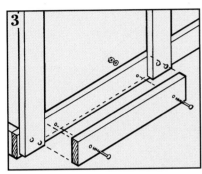

3

Post Blocks: Cut the 2 x 6 into three pieces, to fit snugly between the bottoms of the front corner posts. Bolt the post blocks in place, flush with the floor surface.

Floor: Nail the floorboards in place across the joists. (There will be five for each of the two end compartments and four for the middle compartment.)

Back: Nail the backboards in place, covering back-corner posts.

Front: Feed door slats horizontally into door tracks.

PROCEDURE FOR LIDS

Lids: Construct two of the three lids. Using a drill and galvanized screws, fasten six lid boards to the front and back battens; allow approximately ½ inch between boards. Each lid will measure 36 inches across. Construct the third lid in the same manner, but leave out the two middle boards.

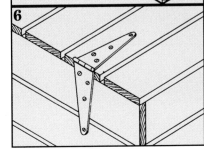

4

5

6

Hatch: Fasten the hatch battens to the two remaining lid boards, one batten approximately 2 inches from the end of the boards and one batten 18 inches from the same end. Fasten the header batten to the boards, 20 inches from the end, just behind the back-hatch batten. Cut between the header batten and the back-hatch batten to separate the hatch. Fasten the two remaining boards and header batten to the partially constructed lid. Hinge the hatch to the lid.

Finish: Hinge the three lids to the bins with the 3-inch hinges, so that they are centered over the compartments. Attach a chain to the bottom of both end lids, at about the middle of the end boards, with screw eyes. Attach a chain to the bottom of both middle-lid end boards, as shown. Mount snap hooks on the ends of the chains. Use pliers to attach screw eyes to the bin partitions, as shown.

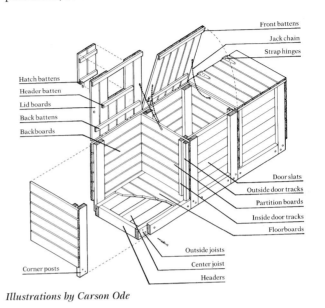

Illustrations by Carson Ode

Labels: Front battens / Jack chain / Strap hinges / Hatch battens / Header batten / Lid boards / Back battens / Backboards / Door slats / Outside door tracks / Partition boards / Inside door tracks / Floorboards / Outside joists / Center joist / Headers / Corner posts

MATERIALS FOR BINS

L U M B E R *
1 pc. 2 x 6 x 108" (center joist)
2 pcs. 2 x 6 x 30" (headers)
2 pcs. 2 x 6 x 111" (outside joists)
2 pcs. 2 x 6 x 141/4" (brace blocks)
4 pcs. 1 x 6 x 33" (short floorboards)
8 pcs. 2 x 6 x 411/2" (corner posts)
24 pcs. 1 x 6 x 36" (partition boards)
6 pcs. 2 x 2 x 34" (inside door tracks)
2 pcs. 2 x 2 x 351/2" (outside doortracks)

1 pc. 2 x 6 x 96" (cut to fit for post blocks)
14 pcs. 2 x 6 x 341/2" (floorboards)
6 pcs. 1 x 6 x 111" (backboards)
18 pcs. 1 x 6 x 351/2" (door slats)
3 pcs. 1 x 3 x 351/2" (door slats)
H A R D W A R E
22 carriage bolts 1/4 x 3 1/2" with nuts and washers
1 box galvanized nails 16d
1 box galvanized nails 8d

MATERIALS FOR LIDS

L U M B E R *
18 pcs. 1 x 6 x 37" (lid boards)
3 pcs. 1 x 2 x 36" (front battens)
3 pcs. 1 x 2 x 34" (back battens)
2 pcs. 1 x 2 x 11 1/4" (hatch battens)
1 pc. 1 x 2 x 22" (header batten)
H A R D W A R E
6 strap hinges 8" (lids)
2 strap hinges 4" (hatch)

4 lengths jack chain, approx. 36" each
8 heavy screw eyes
4 snap hooks
1 box galvanized screws #6 x 1 1/4"
T O O L S
Electric drill
Saw (jigsaw or handsaw)
Hammer
Pliers

*Editor's Note: If you prefer, use untreated pine rather than pressure-treated lumber. Paint with a low-toxicity preservative, such as copper naphthenate.

Compost Bin

Designer Playhouse
PLAN G114

Features at a Glance:

- ✦ Mini-House Design
- ✦ Lots of Natural Light
- ✦ Loft, Ladder and Trap Door!

PLAN G114. *SEE PAGE 92 TO ORDER COMPLETE CONSTRUCTION DRAWINGS FOR THIS PLAN.*

Designed by Conni Cross

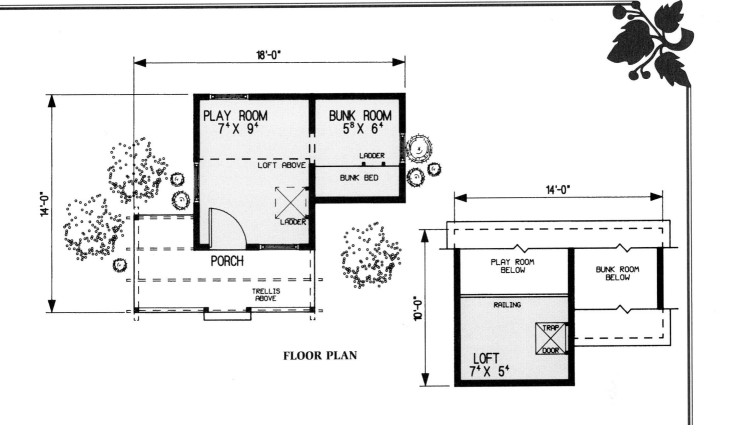

18'-0"

14'-0"

PLAY ROOM
7⁴ X 9⁴

BUNK ROOM
5⁸ X 6⁴

LADDER

LOFT ABOVE

BUNK BED

LADDER

PORCH

TRELLIS
ABOVE

FLOOR PLAN

14'-0"

10'-0"

PLAY ROOM
BELOW

BUNK ROOM
BELOW

RAILING

TRAP
DOOR

LOFT
7⁴ X 5⁴

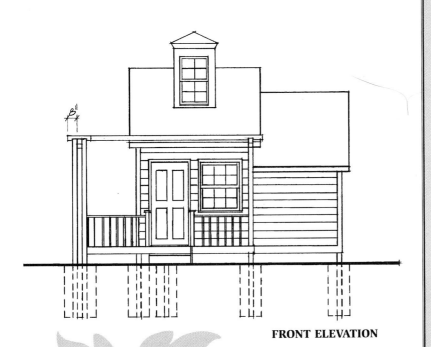

FRONT ELEVATION

*T*his whimsical, scaled-down version of a full-size house makes a dream-come-true playhouse for kids. Designed by Conni Cross, it features a wraparound front porch with a trellis roof, a "real" front door and a loft that can only be reached by a ladder through a trap door! Generous dimensions provide plenty of space for a 7'4"x 9'4" play room and a 5'8"x 6'4" bunk room. A 7'4"x 5'4" loft overlooks the main play area.

Natural light floods all areas of this delightful play center through windows in the play room, bunk room and loft. A sturdy railing borders the loft and built-in bunk beds in the bunk room are ready and waiting for sleep-overs.

Big Kid's Playhouse
PLAN G228

Features at a Glance:

- ✦ Easy to Build
- ✦ High Ceiling
- ✦ Movable

PLAN G228. *SEE PAGE 92 TO ORDER COMPLETE CONSTRUCTION DRAWINGS FOR THIS PLAN.*

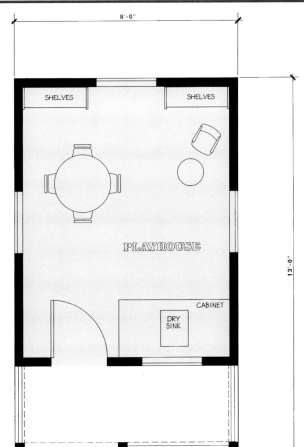

8'-0"

SHELVES   SHELVES

13'-0"

PLAYHOUSE

CABINET

DRY
SINK

FLOOR PLAN

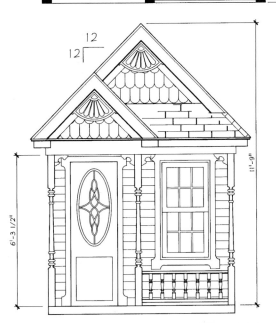

12
12

11'-9"

6'-3 1/2"

FRONT ELEVATION

*T*his large, 180-square-foot, Victorian playhouse is for the kid in all of us. With space enough to hold bunk beds, use it for overnight adventures. Young children will spend hours playing in this little house. Older kids will find it a haven for quiet study or a perfect private retreat. Four windows flood the interior with natural light, and a single-door entrance provides access from the porch. The 8'-1" overall height will accommodate most adults and the addition of electricity and water would expand the versatility of this unit.

Designed on a concrete slab, this playhouse could be placed on a wooden frame for future relocation or change in function after the kids leave home.

Work and/or Play
PLAN G227

Features at a Glance:

- ◆ Dual-Level Roofline
- ◆ Easy to Build
- ◆ 2-in-1 Use

PLAN G227. *SEE PAGE 92 TO ORDER COMPLETE CONSTRUCTION DRAWINGS FOR THIS PLAN.*

Playhouses

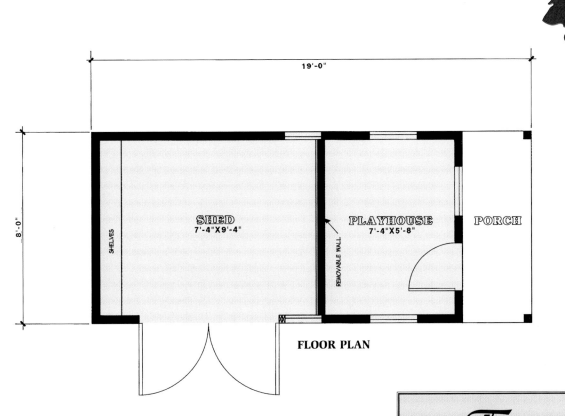

19'-0"

8'-0"

SHELVES

SHED
7'-4"X9'-4"

REMOVABLE WALL

PLAYHOUSE
7'-4"X5'-8"

PORCH

FLOOR PLAN

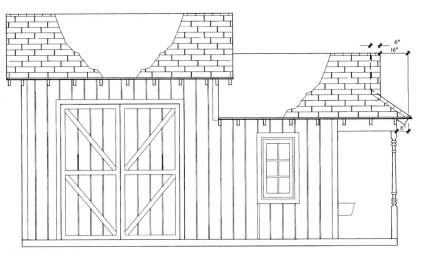

SIDE ELEVATION

6"
16"

6"

The kids will love this one! This functional, practical lawn shed doubles in design and capacity as a delightful playhouse complete with a covered porch, lathe-turned columns and a window box for young gardeners. The higher roofline on the shed gives the playhouse a two-story effect, while the playhouse design gives the simple lawn shed a much more appealing appearance. The shed is accessed through double doors. The playhouse features a single-door entrance from the porch and three bright windows.

The interior wall between the shed and playhouse could be moved another two and a half feet back to make it larger. Or, remove the interior wall completely to use the entire 128-square-foot area exclusively for either the lawn shed or playhouse. The open eaves and porch columns give the structure a country appearance; however, by boxing in the eaves and modifying the columns, you can create just about any style you or the kids like best.

Sail Away
PLAN G229

Features at a Glance:

- ◆ Pure Fun Design
- ◆ Multi-Level
- ◆ Easy to Build

PLAN G229. *SEE PAGE 92 TO ORDER COMPLETE CONSTRUCTION DRAWINGS FOR THIS PLAN.*

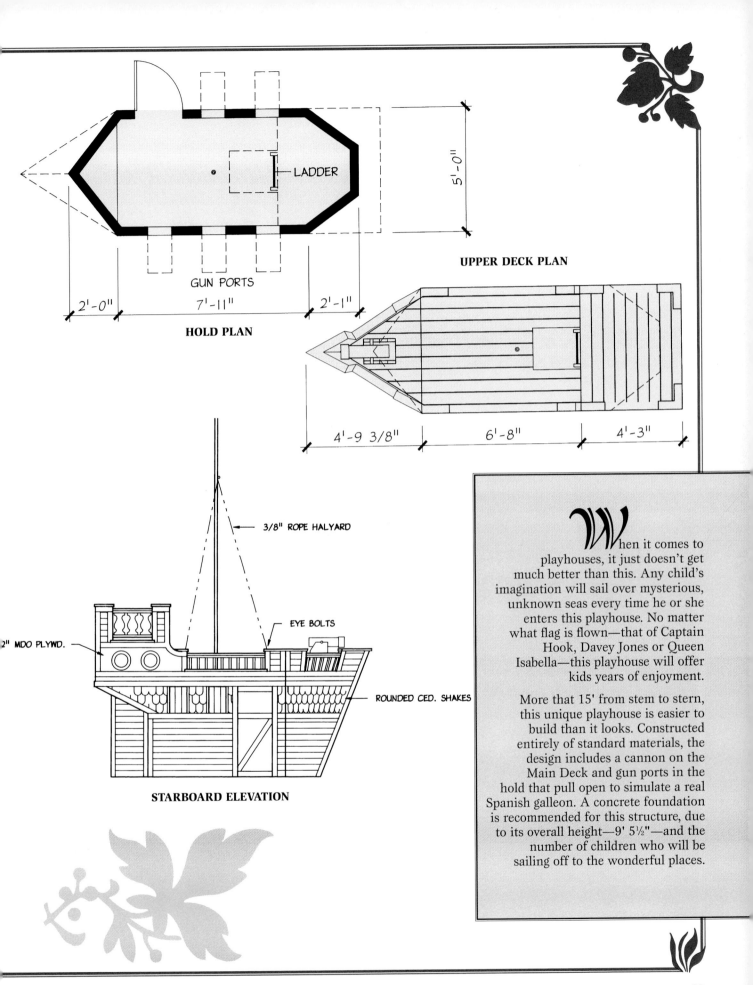

UPPER DECK PLAN

LADDER

GUN PORTS

5'-0"

2'-0"   7'-11"   2'-1"

HOLD PLAN

4'-9 3/8"   6'-8"   4'-3"

3/8" ROPE HALYARD

EYE BOLTS

2" MDO PLYWD.

ROUNDED CED. SHAKES

STARBOARD ELEVATION

When it comes to playhouses, it just doesn't get much better than this. Any child's imagination will sail over mysterious, unknown seas every time he or she enters this playhouse. No matter what flag is flown—that of Captain Hook, Davey Jones or Queen Isabella—this playhouse will offer kids years of enjoyment.

More that 15' from stem to stern, this unique playhouse is easier to build than it looks. Constructed entirely of standard materials, the design includes a cannon on the Main Deck and gun ports in the hold that pull open to simulate a real Spanish galleon. A concrete foundation is recommended for this structure, due to its overall height—9' 5½"—and the number of children who will be sailing off to the wonderful places.

Sunny Craft Cottage
PLAN G109

Features at a Glance:

- ✦ Lots of Windows
- ✦ Vaulted Ceilings
- ✦ Well-Designed Work Space

PLAN G109. *SEE PAGE 92 TO ORDER COMPLETE CONSTRUCTION DRAWINGS FOR THIS PLAN.*

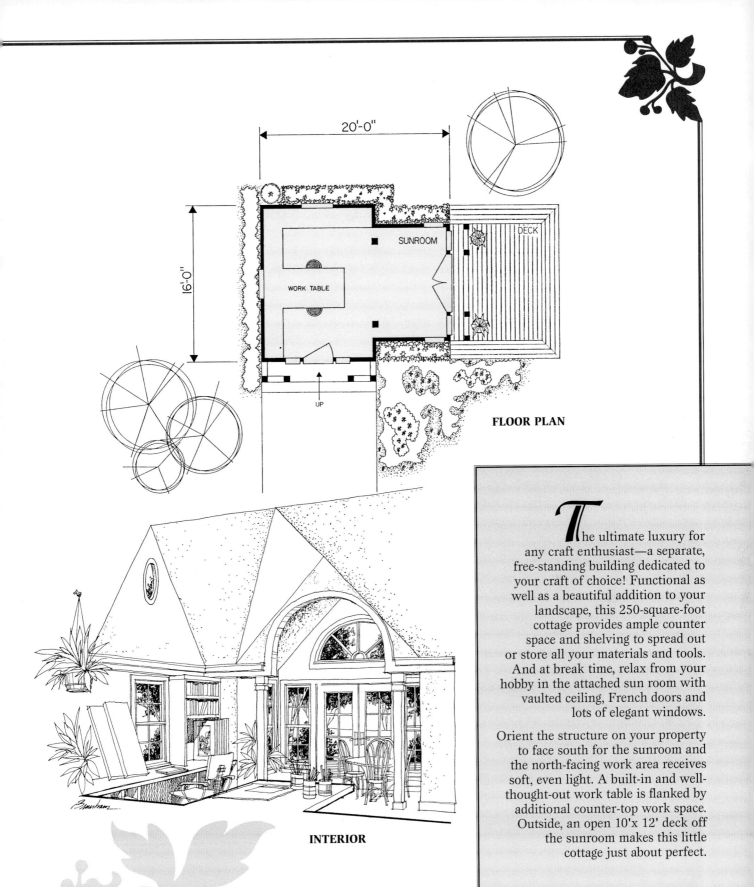

20'-0"

16'-0"

SUNROOM

WORK TABLE

DECK

UP

FLOOR PLAN

INTERIOR

*T*he ultimate luxury for any craft enthusiast—a separate, free-standing building dedicated to your craft of choice! Functional as well as a beautiful addition to your landscape, this 250-square-foot cottage provides ample counter space and shelving to spread out or store all your materials and tools. And at break time, relax from your hobby in the attached sun room with vaulted ceiling, French doors and lots of elegant windows.

Orient the structure on your property to face south for the sunroom and the north-facing work area receives soft, even light. A built-in and well-thought-out work table is flanked by additional counter-top work space. Outside, an open 10'x 12' deck off the sunroom makes this little cottage just about perfect.

Town and Country
PLAN G230

Features at a Glance:

- ✦ Uses All Utilities
- ✦ Large Kitchen Area
- ✦ Half Bath

PLAN G230. *SEE PAGE 92 TO ORDER COMPLETE CONSTRUCTION DRAWINGS FOR THIS PLAN.*

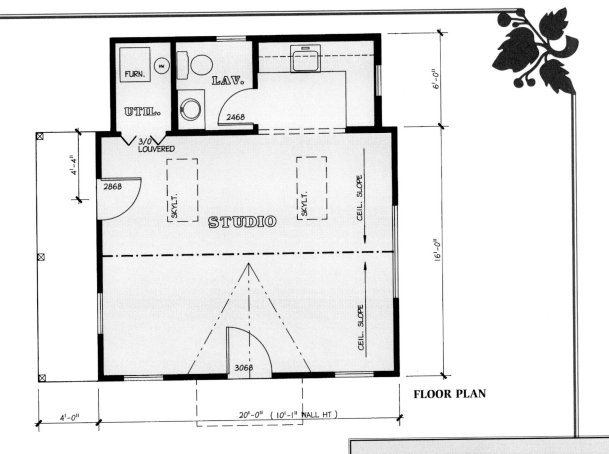

FURN.

HW

UTIL.

LAV.

2468

3/0
LOUVERED

2868

SKYLT.

STUDIO

SKYLT.

CEIL. SLOPE

CEIL. SLOPE

3068

6'-0"

4'-4"

16'-0"

4'-0"

20'-0" (10'-1" WALL HT)

FLOOR PLAN

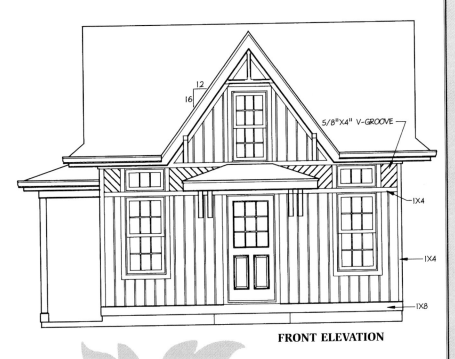

12

16

5/8"X4" V-GROOVE

1X4

1X4

1X8

FRONT ELEVATION

*T*his versatile design features a unique siding pattern: a little bit of country with a pinch of contemporary sophistication. You can build this 440-square-foot, multi-purpose structure on a slab or crawl space or even with a basement! Planned to take advantage of natural light from all sides, this design will make a perfect studio, game room or office. Or, add a shower in the lavatory room and it becomes a guest house.

Features include a half bath, a 6'x18' kitchen—large enough for a stove and refrigerator, and a utility room with ample space for a furnace and hot water tank. With all the amenities provided, you could work or relax here for days without ever leaving! The front porch area is a charming place to relax and put your feet up as you or your guests contemplate the events of the day or prepare for tomorrow.

Teen Territory
PLAN R126

Features at a Glance:

- ✦ Lots of Space
- ✦ Vaulted Ceiling
- ✦ Free-Standing Design

PLAN R126. *SEE PAGE 92 TO ORDER COMPLETE CONSTRUCTION DRAWINGS FOR THIS PLAN.*

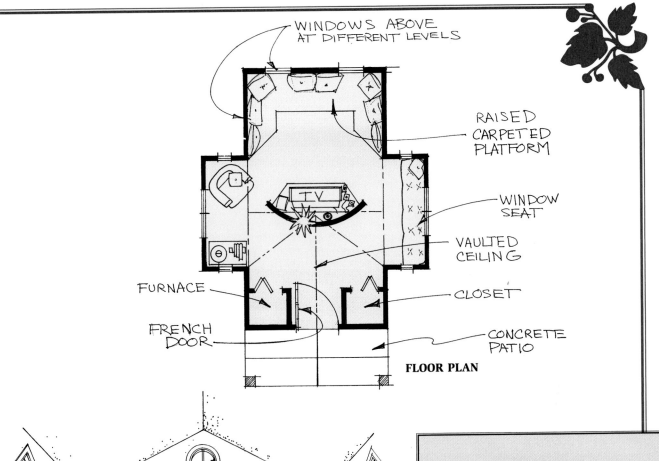

WINDOWS ABOVE
AT DIFFERENT LEVELS

RAISED
CARPETED
PLATFORM

WINDOW
SEAT

VAULTED
CEILING

CLOSET

CONCRETE
PATIO

FURNACE

FRENCH
DOOR

TV

FLOOR PLAN

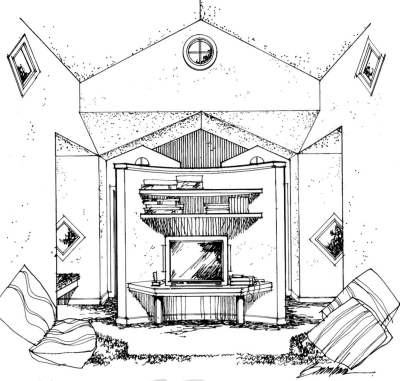

INTERIOR

*L*ucky the teenagers who have the option of staking claim to this private retreat! The overall dimensions of 16'x 22' provide plenty of space for study, TV or just hangin' out. Special features include a raised, carpeted platform in the TV lounge; a comfy window seat for reading or a catnap; a separate niche for electronic games; and a unique, brightly painted graffiti wall in the entryway.

Wired for sound, bright colors and windows in a variety of shapes mark this specially designed, free-standing building as teens-only territory.

Excellent Exercise Cottage
PLAN R129

Features at a Glance:

- ✦ Vaulted Ceiling
- ✦ Sauna and Hot Tub
- ✦ Half-Bath and Mini-Kitchen

PLAN R129. *SEE PAGE 92 TO ORDER COMPLETE*
CONSTRUCTION DRAWINGS FOR THIS PLAN.

Studios and Cottages

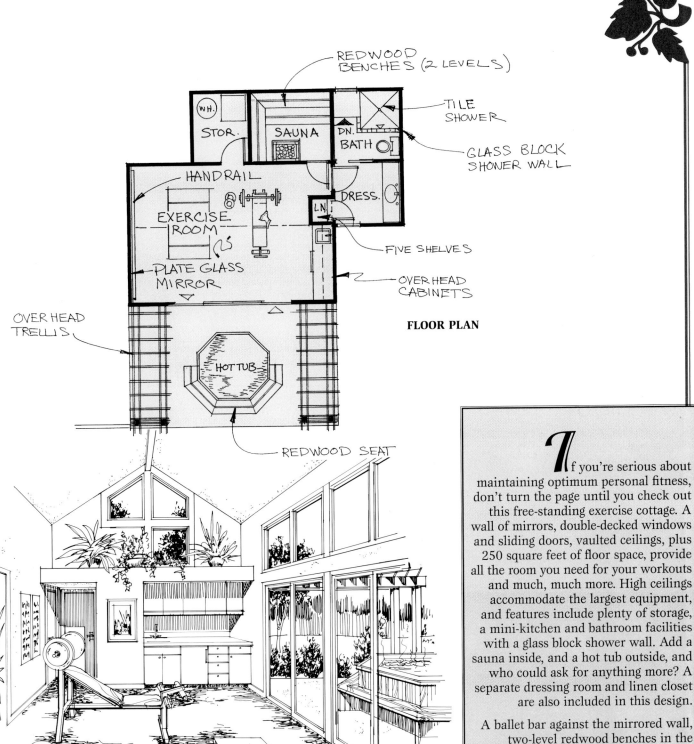

REDWOOD
BENCHES (2 LEVELS)

W.H.

STOR.

SAUNA

TILE
SHOWER

DN.
BATH

GLASS BLOCK
SHOWER WALL

HANDRAIL

EXERCISE
ROOM

DRESS.

LN.

FIVE SHELVES

PLATE GLASS
MIRROR

OVER HEAD
CABINETS

FLOOR PLAN

OVER HEAD
TRELLIS

HOT TUB

REDWOOD SEAT

INTERIOR

*I*f you're serious about maintaining optimum personal fitness, don't turn the page until you check out this free-standing exercise cottage. A wall of mirrors, double-decked windows and sliding doors, vaulted ceilings, plus 250 square feet of floor space, provide all the room you need for your workouts and much, much more. High ceilings accommodate the largest equipment, and features include plenty of storage, a mini-kitchen and bathroom facilities with a glass block shower wall. Add a sauna inside, and a hot tub outside, and who could ask for anything more? A separate dressing room and linen closet are also included in this design.

A ballet bar against the mirrored wall, two-level redwood benches in the sauna and ample storage shelves and cabinets are additional amenities in this inviting personal gym. Overhead trellises provide privacy for both the hot tub and exercise areas.

Swings and Things
PLAN G231

Features at a Glance:

- ✦ Easy to Build
- ✦ Designed for Lots of Use
- ✦ Versatile

PLAN G231. *SEE PAGE 92 TO ORDER COMPLETE CONSTRUCTION DRAWINGS FOR THIS PLAN.*

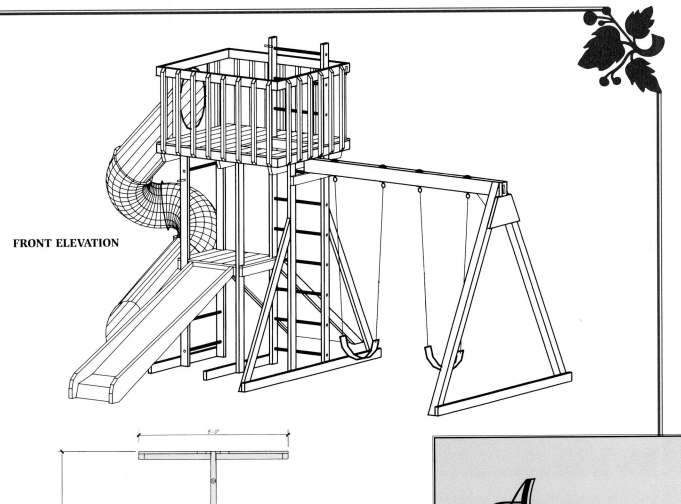

FRONT ELEVATION

TOP VIEW

8'-0"

12'-11 1/2"

5'-0"

OPEN

RAMP

SLIDE

A playset with a little bit of everything. <u>The Swings</u>: This playset is designed to use any of the shelf-style swing units available at your local supplier. <u>The Slides</u>: There are two slides, one regular, the other an enclosed spiral slide to provide added thrills. <u>The Ramp</u>: The ramp is designed for kids who like to climb back up the slide. Now they can climb up the ramp and slide down the slide on the other side. For small children, you can add a knotted rope to help them up. <u>The Eagle's Nest</u>: The climb to the Eagle's Nest will provide your kids with exercise for their muscles and their imagination. Young children will love to switch from one part of this playset to another over and over again.

Swinging Bridge
PLAN G232

Features at a Glance:

- ✦ Variety of Equipment
- ✦ Easy to Build
- ✦ Sturdy

PLAN G232. *SEE PAGE 92 TO ORDER COMPLETE CONSTRUCTION DRAWINGS FOR THIS PLAN.*

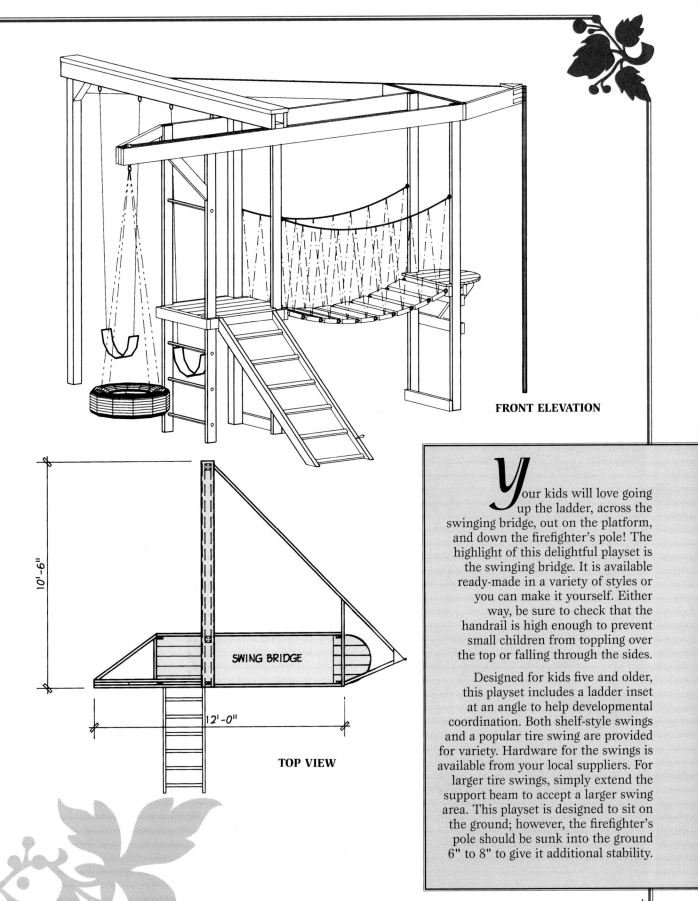

FRONT ELEVATION

10'-6"

SWING BRIDGE

12'-0"

TOP VIEW

*Y*our kids will love going up the ladder, across the swinging bridge, out on the platform, and down the firefighter's pole! The highlight of this delightful playset is the swinging bridge. It is available ready-made in a variety of styles or you can make it yourself. Either way, be sure to check that the handrail is high enough to prevent small children from toppling over the top or falling through the sides.

Designed for kids five and older, this playset includes a ladder inset at an angle to help developmental coordination. Both shelf-style swings and a popular tire swing are provided for variety. Hardware for the swings is available from your local suppliers. For larger tire swings, simply extend the support beam to accept a larger swing area. This playset is designed to sit on the ground; however, the firefighter's pole should be sunk into the ground 6" to 8" to give it additional stability.

Camelot
PLAN G235

Features at a Glance:

- ✦ Innovative Design
- ✦ Uses Standard Materials
- ✦ For Kids of All Ages

PLAN G235. *SEE PAGE 92 TO ORDER COMPLETE CONSTRUCTION DRAWINGS FOR THIS PLAN.*

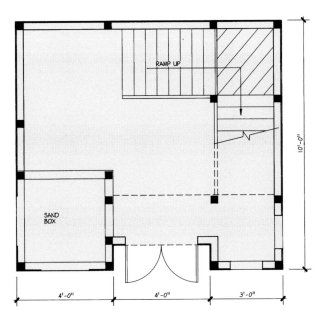

RAMP UP

SAND
BOX

10'-0"

4'-0"   4'-0"   3'-0"

LOWER LEVEL

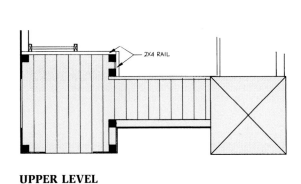

2X4 RAIL

UPPER LEVEL

FRONT ELEVATION

*L*ords and ladies, knights and evil-doers—this playhouse has everything except a fire-breathing dragon! Your children will spend hours re-enacting the days of Kings and Queens and Knights of the Round Table.

Surprisingly easy to build, this playset right out of King Arthur's Court uses standard materials. One corner of the playhouse holds a 4'x4' sandbox. A stairway leads to a 3'x3' tower with its own catwalk. The area under the stairway could be enclosed to make a storage room for toys . . . or a dungeon to hold the captured Black Knight. The double castle doors can be fitted with standard hardware, but wrought-iron hinges will make this innovative playhouse look even more like a castle.

The Lookout
PLAN G234

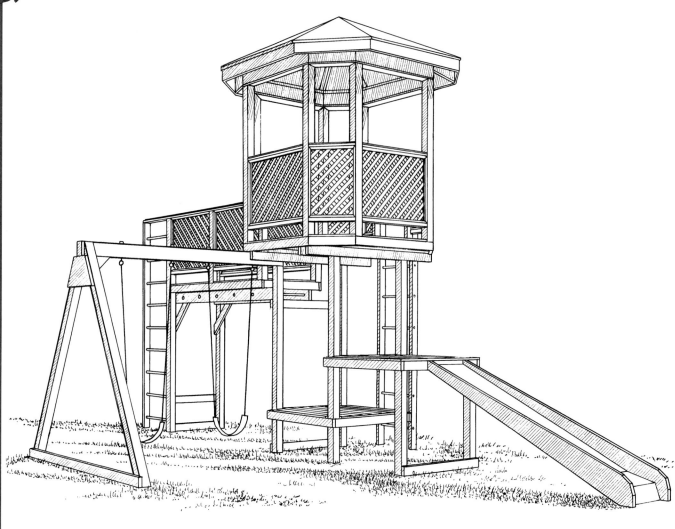

Features at a Glance:

- ✦ Adjustable Equipment
- ✦ Easy to Build
- ✦ Versatile

PLAN G234. *SEE PAGE 92 TO ORDER COMPLETE CONSTRUCTION DRAWINGS FOR THIS PLAN.*

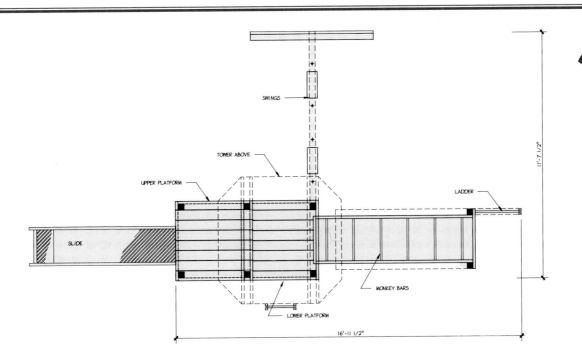

SWINGS

TOWER ABOVE

UPPER PLATFORM

LADDER

SLIDE

MONKEY BARS

LOWER PLATFORM

11'-7 1/2"

16'-11 1/2"

REAR ELEVATION

A play house, a tree house, a lookout tower . . . your children will invent many uses for this mini-gazebo perched an exciting 7'-10½" above the ground. It's large enough for a small table and chairs for a picnic or a Mad Hatter's tea party. Or, spread out some sleeping bags and invite friends for an overnight adventure — but no sleep-walking! The ladder, swings and slide all add to the fun and can be modified to accommodate the ages of your children.

If you have a full-size gazebo on your site, or plan to build one, you could use a similar design in the railings for both units for a surprising "double-take" effect.

Rain or Shine Pool Cabana
PLAN G110

Features at a Glance:

+ Multi-Purpose
+ Large Covered Area
+ Lovely Exterior

PLAN G110. *SEE PAGE 92 TO ORDER COMPLETE CONSTRUCTION DRAWINGS FOR THIS PLAN.*

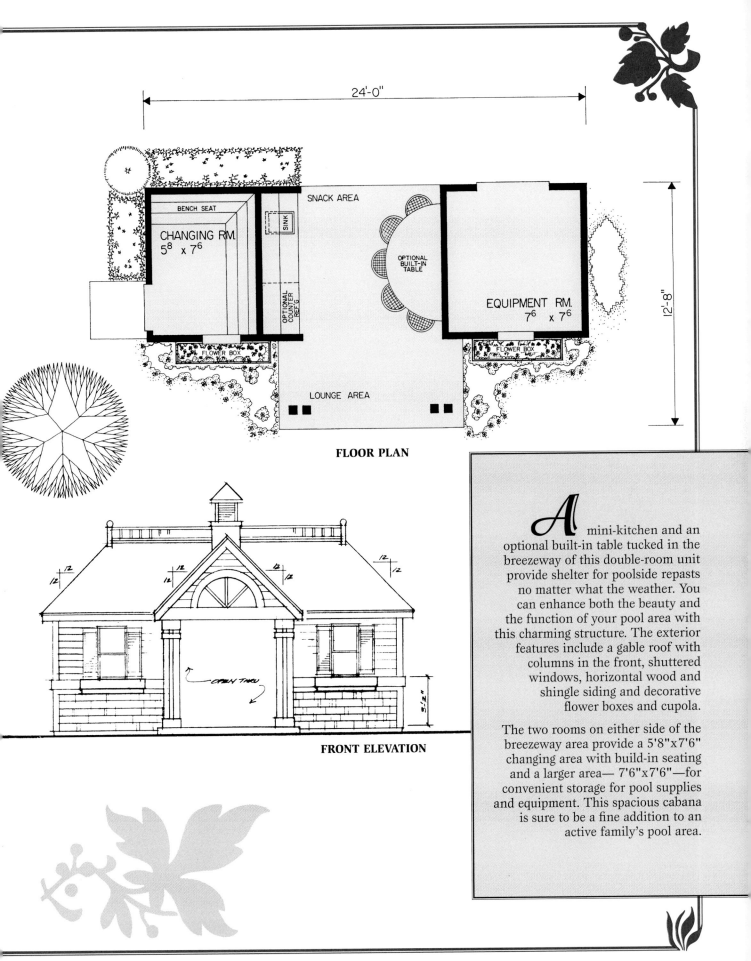

24'-0"

12'-8"

BENCH SEAT

CHANGING RM.
5⁸ x 7⁶

SINK

SNACK AREA

OPTIONAL
BUILT-IN
TABLE

OPTIONAL
COUNTER
REF'G

EQUIPMENT RM.
7⁶ x 7⁶

FLOWER BOX

FLOWER BOX

LOUNGE AREA

FLOOR PLAN

12 12 12 12 12 12

OPEN THRU

3'-2"

FRONT ELEVATION

A mini-kitchen and an optional built-in table tucked in the breezeway of this double-room unit provide shelter for poolside repasts no matter what the weather. You can enhance both the beauty and the function of your pool area with this charming structure. The exterior features include a gable roof with columns in the front, shuttered windows, horizontal wood and shingle siding and decorative flower boxes and cupola.

The two rooms on either side of the breezeway area provide a 5'8"x7'6" changing area with build-in seating and a larger area— 7'6"x7'6"—for convenient storage for pool supplies and equipment. This spacious cabana is sure to be a fine addition to an active family's pool area.

Triple Duty
PLAN G239

Features at a Glance:

- ✦ Lots of Built-ins
- ✦ Compact Size
- ✦ Elegant Lines

PLAN G239. *SEE PAGE 92 TO ORDER COMPLETE CONSTRUCTION DRAWINGS FOR THIS PLAN.*

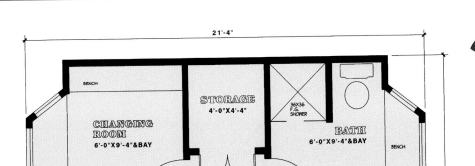

21'-4"

BENCH

CHANGING
ROOM
6'-0"X9'-4"&BAY

STORAGE
4'-0"X4'-4"

36X36
F.G.
SHOWER

BATH
6'-0"X9'-4"&BAY

BENCH

BENCH

TOWELS

TOWELS

ROD & SHELF

18'-0"

FLOOR PLAN

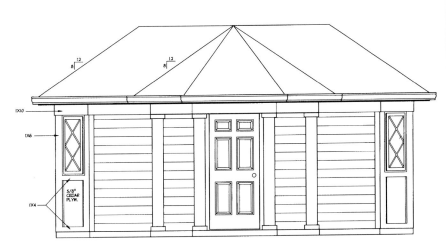

12
8

12
8

1X10

1X6

5/8"
CEDAR
PLYW.

1X4

FRONT ELEVATION

A changing room, a summer kitchen, and an elegant porch for shade. Add the convenience of bathroom facilities and you're set for outdoor living all summer long. This pool pavilion is designed to provide maximum function in a small area and features built-in benches, shelves, hanging rods and a separate linen closet for towels.

The opaque diamond-patterned windows decorate the exterior of the 10'x6'8" changing area and the mirror-image bath. The bath could also be made into a kitchen area, then simply add a sliding window to allow easy passage of refreshments to your family and guests at poolside. When you've had enough sun or socializing, recline in the shade under the columned porch and enjoy a good book or a nap.

Quick Change Architecture
PLAN G238

Features at a Glance:

- ◆ Optional Uses
- ◆ Covered Walkway
- ◆ Impressive Design

PLAN G238. *SEE PAGE 92 TO ORDER COMPLETE CONSTRUCTION DRAWINGS FOR THIS PLAN.*

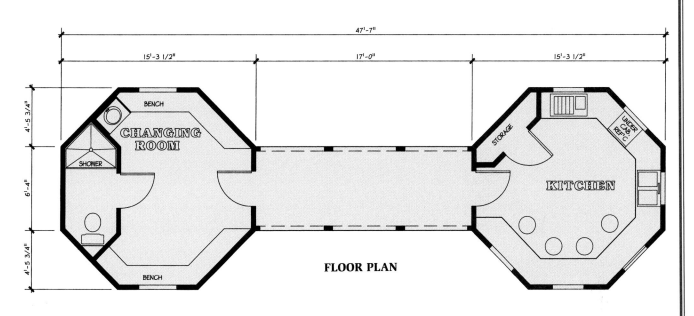

FLOOR PLAN

(Dimensions shown: 47'-7", 15'-3 1/2", 17'-0", 15'-3 1/2", 4'-5 3/4", 6'-4", 4'-5 3/4")

Labels in plan: CHANGING ROOM, BENCH, SHOWER, BENCH, STORAGE, KITCHEN, UNDER CAB REF-C

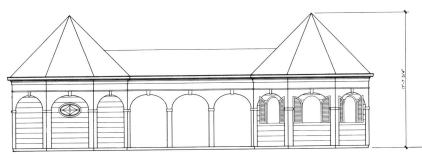

FRONT ELEVATION

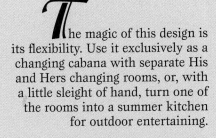

The magic of this design is its flexibility. Use it exclusively as a changing cabana with separate His and Hers changing rooms, or, with a little sleight of hand, turn one of the rooms into a summer kitchen for outdoor entertaining.

As changing rooms, each eight-sided area includes built-in benches and private bathroom facilities. The 15'-3.5"x 15'-3.5" kitchen option includes a stove, refrigerator, food preparation area and a storage pantry. A shuttered window poolside provides easy access to serve your guests across the counter. Linking these two areas is a covered walkway which serves as a shaded picnic area, or a convenient place to get out of the sun. Columns, arches and stained-glass windows provide a touch of grandeur to this fun and functional poolside design.

Starlight Spa
PLAN G240

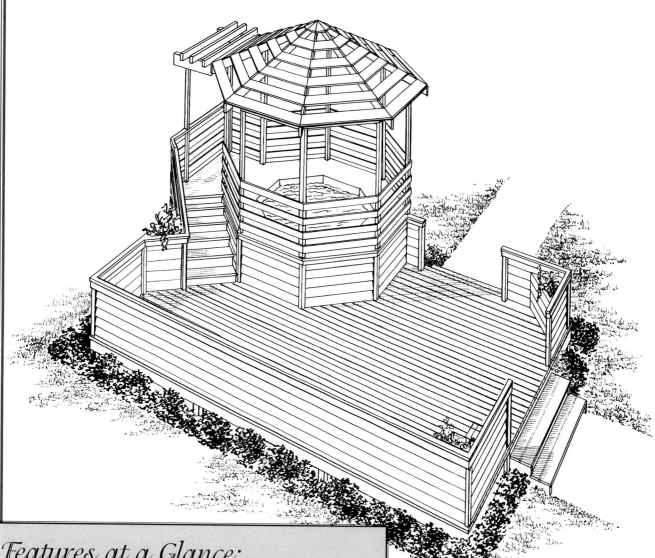

Features at a Glance:

- ◆ Dual Levels
- ◆ Trellis or Solid Roof
- ◆ Accommodates a Variety of Spa Styles

PLAN G240. *SEE PAGE 92 TO ORDER COMPLETE CONSTRUCTION DRAWINGS FOR THIS PLAN.*

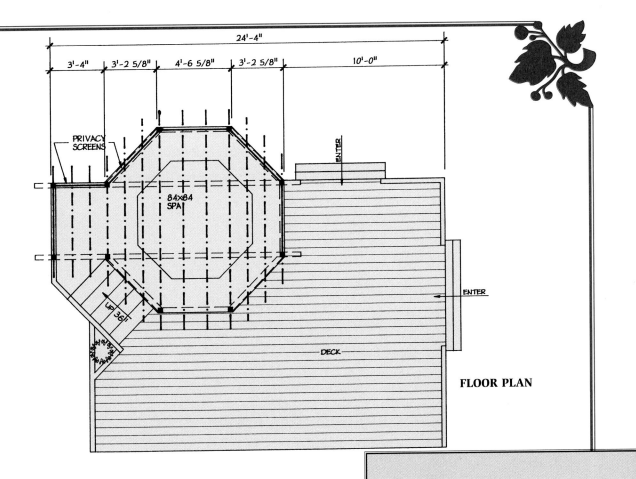

24'-4"

3'-4" | 3'-2 5/8" | 4'-6 5/8" | 3'-2 5/8" | 10'-0"

PRIVACY
SCREENS

ENTER

84x84
SPA

UP 36"

ENTER

DECK

FLOOR PLAN

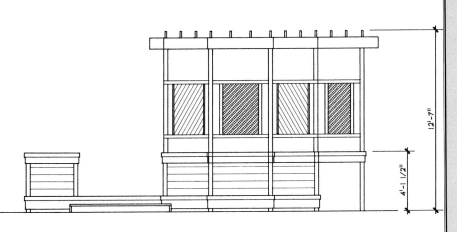

12'-7"

4'-1 1/2"

REAR ELEVATION

*S*ecluded enough for privacy, yet open enough to view the night sky through a curtain of vines on the trellis roof, this private outdoor spa has its own deck with built-in benches and planters. Approximately 280 square feet in area, the deck of this outstanding unit offers plenty of space to entertain friends and family. In the design shown, three steps lead up from the ground to the deck, and six additional steps lead up to the 84"x84" spa area. Patterned screens and a trellis roof provide privacy.

You can place this spa adjacent to your house for convenient access, or install it as a free-standing unit in a secluded area of your property. Easy to build, this design will accommodate a spa of almost any style. The trellis roof can also be modified to a solid roof style or eliminated completely.

Whirlpool/Sauna Oasis
PLAN G112

Features at a Glance:

- ✦ Spacious Deck Area
- ✦ Dry-Heat Sauna
- ✦ Revitalizing Whirlpool Spa

PLAN G112. *SEE PAGE 92 TO ORDER COMPLETE CONSTRUCTION DRAWINGS FOR THIS PLAN.*

Trellises

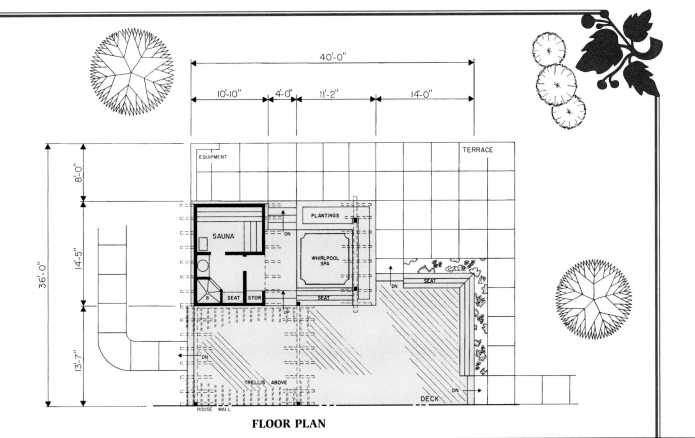

FLOOR PLAN

Dimensions shown: 40'-0", 10'-10", 4'-0", 11'-2", 14'-0", 8'-0", 14'-5", 36'-0", 13'-7"

Labels: EQUIPMENT, TERRACE, SAUNA, PLANTINGS, WHIRLPOOL SPA, DN, UP, SEAT, STOR, S, TRELLIS ABOVE, HOUSE WALL, DECK

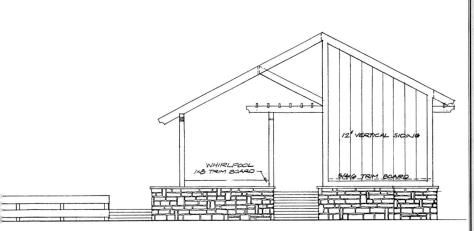

12" VERTICAL SIDING

WHIRLPOOL
1x8 TRIM BOARD

5/4x6 TRIM BOARD

REAR ELEVATION

A true oasis in Webster's second definition of the word—any place offering welcome relief from difficulty—this relaxing addition promises respite from the hectic world outside. This perfect combination of sauna and whirlpool spa is joined to your house by wood decking and a sun- (or moon-) filtering trellis. The dry-heat sauna has planked seating and a dressing area with sink and shower and a bench seat. A small attached storage room accommodates supplies and equipment.

The revitalizing whirlpool spa features raised planters on two sides for added privacy and a long bench seat. The adjoining, spacious deck area—13'7"x40'—features additional bench seating along two sides. The simple lines and open design allow this plan to blend perfectly with any style or type of house.

Covered Outdoor Kitchen
PLAN R127

Features at a Glance:

- ✦ Complete Mini-Kitchen
- ✦ Large Brick Barbecue Grill
- ✦ Optional Screen Room

PLAN R127. *SEE PAGE 92 TO ORDER COMPLETE
CONSTRUCTION DRAWINGS FOR THIS PLAN.*

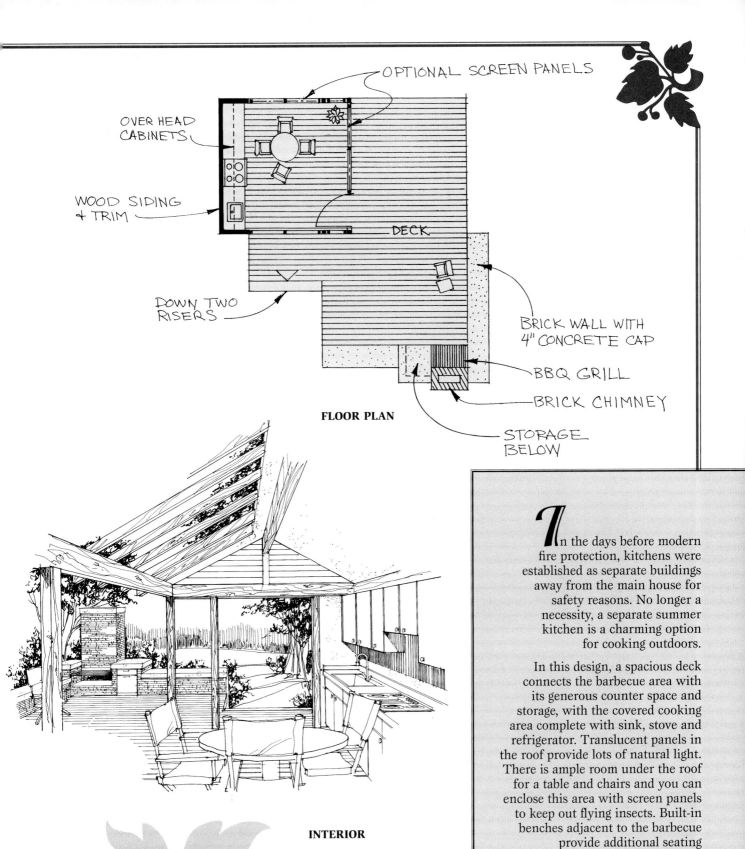

OPTIONAL SCREEN PANELS

OVER HEAD CABINETS

WOOD SIDING + TRIM

DECK

DOWN TWO RISERS

BRICK WALL WITH 4" CONCRETE CAP

BBQ GRILL

BRICK CHIMNEY

STORAGE BELOW

FLOOR PLAN

INTERIOR

*I*n the days before modern fire protection, kitchens were established as separate buildings away from the main house for safety reasons. No longer a necessity, a separate summer kitchen is a charming option for cooking outdoors.

In this design, a spacious deck connects the barbecue area with its generous counter space and storage, with the covered cooking area complete with sink, stove and refrigerator. Translucent panels in the roof provide lots of natural light. There is ample room under the roof for a table and chairs and you can enclose this area with screen panels to keep out flying insects. Built-in benches adjacent to the barbecue provide additional seating or serving space.

Y'all Come!
PLAN G241

Features at a Glance:

- ✦ Outdoor Kitchen
- ✦ Plenty of Built-ins
- ✦ Large Screened Room

PLAN G241. *SEE PAGE 92 TO ORDER COMPLETE CONSTRUCTION DRAWINGS FOR THIS PLAN.*

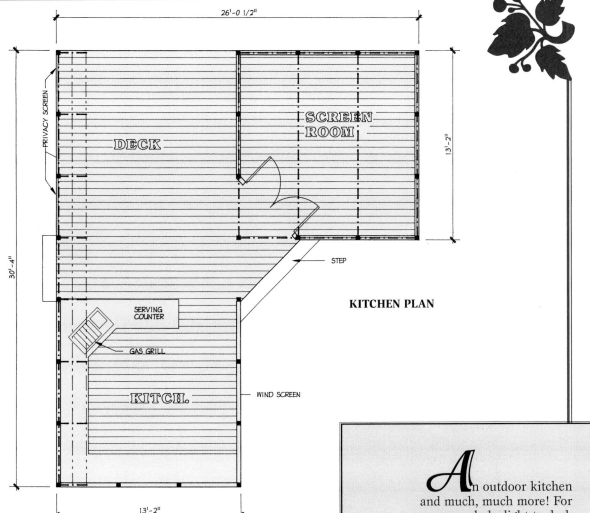

26'-0 1/2"

PRIVACY SCREEN

DECK

SCREEN ROOM

13'-2"

30'-4"

STEP

KITCHEN PLAN

SERVING COUNTER

GAS GRILL

KITCH.

WIND SCREEN

13'-2"

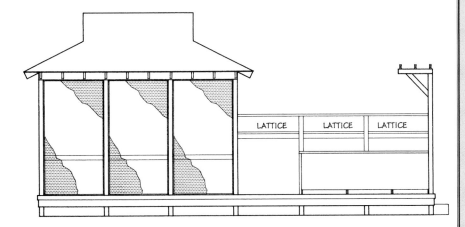

LATTICE   LATTICE   LATTICE

REAR ELEVATION

*A*n outdoor kitchen and much, much more! For year-round, daylight-to-dark entertaining, consider this large outdoor entertainment unit. Nearly 700 square feet of floor space includes a deck for sunbathing by day or dancing under the stars after sundown. A 13' x 13'-2" screened room provides a pest-free environment for cards or conversation. And, the Cookout Chef will rule with a flair over a full-service kitchen area that may include a grill, wet bar, sink, refrigerator and ample room for storage.

You can locate this versatile structure adjacent to your pool, or place it as a free-standing unit wherever your landscape and site plan allow. Select material for the railings and privacy screens in patterns to match or complement your home.

Garden Glider
PLAN G237

Features at a Glance:

- ✦ Clever Styling
- ✦ Functional
- ✦ Two Seating Options

PLAN G237. *SEE PAGE 92 TO ORDER COMPLETE CONSTRUCTION DRAWINGS FOR THIS PLAN.*

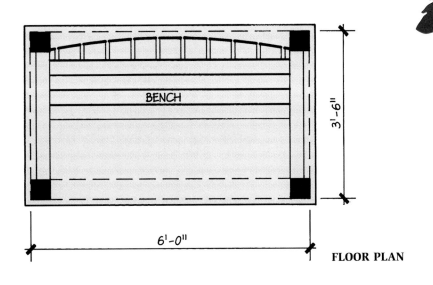

BENCH

3'-6"

6'-0"

FLOOR PLAN

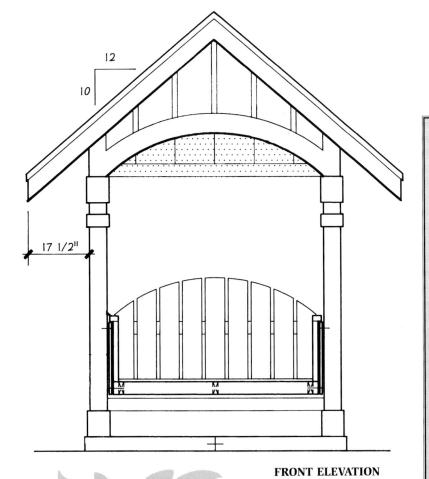

12

10

17 1/2"

FRONT ELEVATION

$\mathcal{Y}$ou can create a cozy shaded nook for reading or relaxing with this appealing strombella. It's simple to build as a glider or with a fixed seat. Either option provides ample room for two or three people to sit comfortably. Both designs use standard materials. For a fixed unit, attach it to a cement slab. To make it movable, use a wood base. Cover the roof with basic asphalt or fiberglass shingles, or use cedar shake shingles to enhance the appearance.

Victorian Grace
PLAN G236

Features at a Glance:

+ Novel Design
+ Victorian Style
+ Functional

PLAN G236. *SEE PAGE 92 TO ORDER COMPLETE CONSTRUCTION DRAWINGS FOR THIS PLAN.*

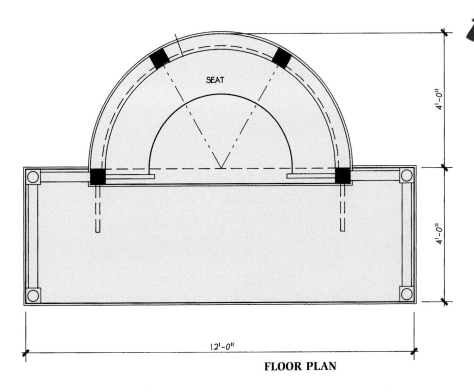

FLOOR PLAN

SEAT

4'-0"

4'-0"

12'-0"

7 | 12

FRONT ELEVATION

*A*n accent to gracious living, this classic strombrella will create an elegant focal point in any garden or landscape. Evoking memories of a more slowly paced era, the design is similar to those built in the late 1800s. The bench is large enough to seat up to six people. To increase its function, a half-round pole table could be added to provide a small picnic area or a nook for reading, cards or quiet conversation. The mill work can be purchased from your local supplier or from the manufacturer listed on the construction drawings. The generous entrance is 4' wide which could provide space for additional seating if needed. You can build this structure with a wood base to allow for movable feasts, or secure it to a slab to make it permanent.

Sun and Shade
Plan G242

FRONT ELEVATION

3'-6"

4'-0"

4'-0"

Features at a Glance...

- ✦ Sunburst Design
- ✦ Three Trellis Plans
- ✦ Includes Matching Fence

PLAN G242. *SEE PAGE 92 TO ORDER COMPLETE CONSTRUCTION DRAWINGS FOR THIS PLAN.*

A distinctive sunburst pattern is repeated in each element of this attractive and versatile 8' garden arbor. Train your favorite vines over the slat roof to provide shade for the flower beds below or for the roses climbing along the 1x6 slat-fence extensions. Also included in this package are plans for a 4' corner trellis which can be used to extend the sunburst pattern to other areas of your landscape and serve as an accent in flower beds or planters. This arbor—with its sunburst effect—offers a warm and welcoming focal point to any yard or garden area.

Trellis Bench
PLAN G243

ARBOR FRONT

BENCH FRONT

Build this impressive arbor to cover a garden path or walkway. Add the matching bench inside the arbor as a plant shelf or to provide shaded seating. Use the bench outside as an accent to both the arbor and the surrounding landscape. The 7'-11" patterned back and 5'-11"x 8'10½" trellis roof are ideal for climbing vines or roses, giving this beautiful arbor even more of a garden effect.

The 8'-11" bench is wide enough to seat four or five adults comfortably. The latticework design is repeated on the back and sides of the bench. The arbor is designed to sit on a slab, or you can sink the support columns right into the ground using pressure-treated materials.

Features at a Glance...

◆ Unique Design
◆ Movable Bench
◆ Easy to Build

PLAN G243. *SEE PAGE 92 TO ORDER COMPLETE CONSTRUCTION DRAWINGS FOR THIS PLAN.*

A Bridge to the Past
PLAN G244

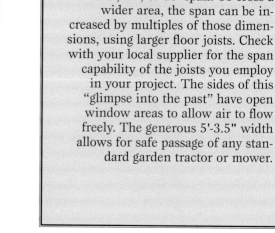

END ELEVATION

SIDE ELEVATION

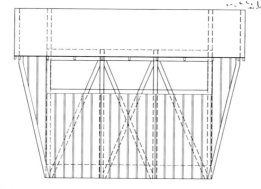

Features at a Glance...

- ✦ Historic Design
- ✦ Expandable Dimensions
- ✦ Decorative and Functional

PLAN G244. *SEE PAGE 92 TO ORDER COMPLETE CONSTRUCTION DRAWINGS FOR THIS PLAN.*

ostalgia unlimited— this romantic covered bridge will recreate a unique link to history on your site. It is patterned after functional bridges built in the 1700s and 1800s, which were intended to provide a dry resting place for weary travelers. This current-day design offers expandable dimensions for a 12', 14', or 16' span. To cross a wider area, the span can be increased by multiples of those dimensions, using larger floor joists. Check with your local supplier for the span capability of the joists you employ in your project. The sides of this "glimpse into the past" have open window areas to allow air to flow freely. The generous 5'-3.5" width allows for safe passage of any standard garden tractor or mower.

Beauty and the Bridge
PLAN G245

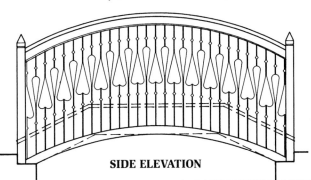

SIDE ELEVATION

Combine form, function and beauty in this appealing bridge to enhance your landscape and provide easy passage over wet or rocky terrain. Entrance and exit ramps at either end of the bridge replicate the gentle arch of the handrail. The plans for this functional addition show how to build 6', 8' or 10' spans to meet your needs. The decorative railing pattern will add a touch of elegance and charm to any site.

Features at a Glance...

- ◆ Functional
- ◆ Decorative
- ◆ Three Span Lengths

PLAN G245. *SEE PAGE 92 TO ORDER COMPLETE CONSTRUCTION DRAWINGS FOR THIS PLAN.*

Yard & Garden Structures Blueprint Package

The blueprint package for these inspiring Yard and Garden Structures contains everything you need to plan and build the outdoor amenity of your choice. Some of the more complicated gazebos and lawn shed packages will have several sheets to thoroughly explain how the structure will go together. The simpler structures such as bridges and arbors have fewer sheets. To help you further understand the process of constructing an outdoor structure, we also offer a separate package—Gazebo Construction Details—which outlines general information for construction of gazebos and similar outdoor amenities. Included are numerous illustrations, an explanation of building terms, and general tips and hints to make your building project progress smoothly.

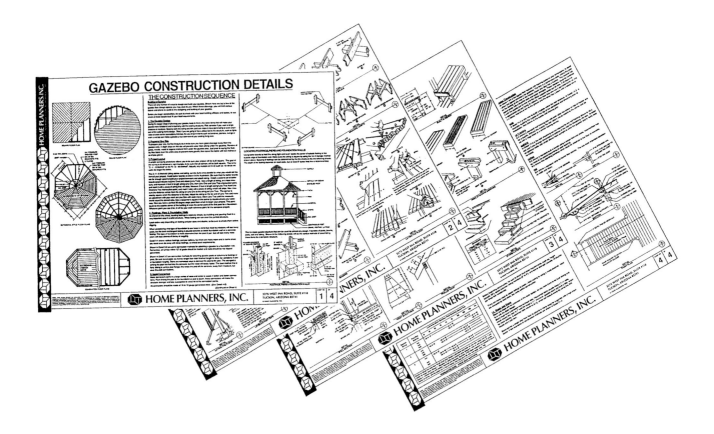

Gazebo Construction Details

This set of 24"x18" sheets contains a wealth of valuable information for gazebos and other outdoor building projects. Included are the steps of the building process; an explanation of terms; details for locating footings, piers, and foundations; information about attaching posts to piers or footings; creating free-standing benches; and much, much more. These sheets will facilitate many different outdoor construction projects for the do-it-yourselfer and will make working with contractors and subcontractors more comfortable.

Only $14.95

Or buy the Complete Construction Set which includes plans for the Yard or Garden Structure of your choice plus the Gazebo Construction Details—see page 94 for price information.

Yard and Garden Structure Plans

The plans for our Yard and Garden Structures have been custom-created by a professional designer. Among the helpful sheets for building your structure may be such information as:

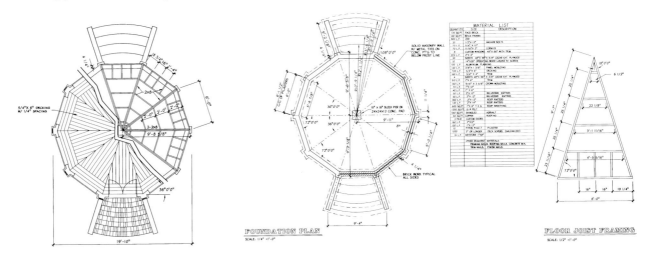

Floor Plan

Done in ½" = 1' scale, this sheet shows the exact floor plan of the structure with dimensions, flooring patterns and window and door call-outs. Details found on other sheets may also be referenced on this sheet.

Foundation and Joist Details/Materials List

This schematic of the foundation and floor and rafter joists, done in ¼" = 1' or ½" = 1' scale, gives dimensions and shows how to pour or construct the foundation and flooring components. The materials list is invaluable for estimating and planning work and acts as an accurate "shopping list" for the do-it-yourselfer.

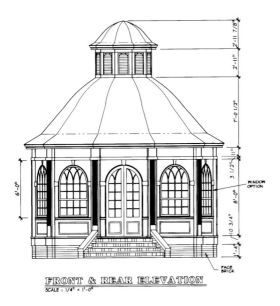

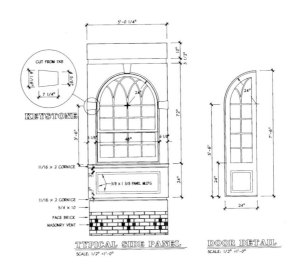

Elevations and Framing Plans/Wall Sections

Shown in ¼" = 1' or ½" = 1' scale, these helpful drawings show various views of the structure plus a complete framing plan for the flooring. Wall sections provide stud sizes, connector types, and rafter and roofing materials. They may also show mouldings or other trim pieces.

Details

Cut-out details, shown in ¼" = 1' or 1" = 1' scale, are given for items such as pilaster framing, doors, side panels and rafter profiles. These details provide additional information and enhance your understanding of other aspects of the plans.

TO ORDER, CALL TOLL FREE 1-800-521-6797

Yard and Garden Structures Price Index

Price Index

Yard and Garden Structures

Price Group	GD1	GD2	GD3	GD4	GD5	GD6
1 Set Custom Plan	$20	$30	$40	$50	$75	$85

Additional Identical Sets . . . . $10 each
Reverse Sets (mirror image) . . . . $10 each

Gazebo Construction Details

1 set Generic Gazebo Construction Details . . . . $14.95 each

Complete Construction Package

Price Group	GD1	GD2	GD3	GD4	GD5	GD6
1 Set Custom Plans, plus 1 Set Gazebo Construction Details	$30	$40	$50	$60	$85	$95

HOUSE PLAN	PAGE	PRICE	HOUSE PLAN	PAGE	PRICE
G246	12	GD2	G109	54	GD3
G218	14	GD2	G230	56	GD3
G221	16	GD2	R126	58	GD5
G108	18	GD1	R129	60	GD6
G217	20	GD2	G231	62	GD1
G220	22	GD1	G232	64	GD1
G219	24	GD1	G235	66	GD3
G216	26	GD2	G234	68	GD2
G215	28	GD2	G110	70	GD3
G107	30	GD2	G239	72	GD3
G247	32	GD2	G238	74	GD4
G222	34	GD3	G240	76	GD2
G223	36	GD3	G112	78	GD2
G226	38	GD3	R127	80	GD5
G225	40	GD3	G241	82	GD5
G224	42	GD2	G237	84	GD2
G248	44	incl.	G236	86	GD2
G114	46	GD2	G242	88	GD1
G228	48	GD2	G243	89	GD1
G227	50	GD3	G244	90	GD2
G229	52	GD3	G245	91	GD2

Yard and Garden Structures
Blueprint Order Form

TO ORDER: Find the Plan number in the Plans Index (opposite). Consult the Price Schedule (opposite) to determine the price of your plan, adding any additional or reverse sets you desire. Or specify the Complete Construction Package, which contains 1 set of Custom Plans of your choice, plus 1 set of Gazebo Construction Details. Complete the order form on this page and mail with your check or money order. Please include the correct postage and handling fees. If you prefer, you can also use a credit card and call our toll-free number, 1-800-521-6797, to place your order.

Our Service Policy
We try to process and ship every order from our office within 48 hours. For this reason, we won't send a formal notice acknowledging receipt of your order.

Our Exchange Policy
Because we produce and ship plans in response to individual orders, we cannot honor requests for refunds. However, you can exchange your entire order of blueprints, including a single set if you order just one, for a set of another design. All exchanges carry an additional fee of $15.00 plus $8.00 postage and handling if they're sent Regular Service; $12.00 via 2nd Day Air; $22.00 via Next Day Air.

About Reverse Blueprints
If you want to install your structure in reverse of the plan as shown, we will include an extra set of blueprints with the images reversed for an additional fee of $10.00. Although callouts and lettering appear backward, reverses will prove useful as a visual aid if you decide to flop the plan.

How Many Blueprints Do You Need?
To study your favorite design, one set of blueprints may be sufficient. On the other hand, if you plan to use contractors or subcontractors to complete the project, you will probably need more sets. Use the checklist below to estimate the number of sets you'll need.
_____ Owner
_____ Contractor or Subcontractor
_____ Building Materials Supplier
_____ Lender or Mortgage Source, if applicable
_____ Community Building Department for Permits
        (sometimes requires 2 sets)
_____ Subdivision Committee, if any
_____ Total Number of Sets

Blueprint Hotline
Call Toll Free 1-800-521-6797. We'll ship your order the following business day if you call us by 4:00 p.m. Eastern Time. When you order by phone, please be prepared to give us the Order Form Key Number shown in the box at the bottom of the Order Form.

By FAX: Copy the order form at right and send on our FAX line: 1-800-224-6699 or 1-602-297-9937.

Canadian Customers
Order Toll Free 1-800-561-4169
For faster service and plans that are modified for building in Canada, customers may now call in orders directly to our Canadian supplier of plans and charge the purchase to a charge card. Or, you may complete the order form at right, adding 40% to all prices and mail in Canadian funds to:
    The Plan Centre
    20 Cedar Street North
    Kitchener, Ontario N2H 2W8

By Fax: Copy the Order Form at right and send it via our Canadian FAX line: 1-519-743-1282.

HOME PLANNERS, INC.
3275 WEST INA ROAD, SUITE 110
TUCSON, ARIZONA 85741

Please rush me the following:
_____ Set(s) of Custom Plan _____
    (See index and Price Schedule) $ _____
_____ Additional identical blueprints in
    same order $10 per set. $ _____
_____ Reverse blueprints at $10 per set. $ _____
_____ Sets of Gazebo Construction Details
    at $14.95 per set. $ _____
_____ Sets of Complete Construction Package (Best Buy!)
    Includes Custom Plan _____
    Plus Gazebo Construction Details $ _____

POSTAGE AND HANDLING		
Carrier Delivery (Requires street address—No P.O Boxes)		
• Regular Service (Allow 4-6 days delivery)	$ 8.00	$ _____
• 2nd Day Air (Allow 2-3 days delivery)	$12.00	$ _____
• Next Day Air (Allow 1 day delivery)	$22.00	$ _____
Post Office Delivery If no street address available. (Allow 4-6 days delivery)	$10.00	$ _____
Overseas Delivery	Phone, FAX or Mail for Quote	

POSTAGE (from box above) $ _____

SUB-TOTAL $ _____

SALES TAX (Arizona residents add 5% sales tax; Michigan residents add 6% sales tax. $ _____

TOTAL (Sub-total and Tax) $ _____

YOUR ADDRESS (please print)
Name _____
Street _____
City _____ State _____ ZIP _____
Daytime telephone number (_____) _____

FOR CREDIT CARD ORDERS ONLY
Please fill in the information below:

Credit card number _____

Exp. Date: Month/Year _____

Check One: ☐ Visa ☐ MasterCard ☐ Discover Card

Signature _____

ORDER TOLL FREE
1-800-521-6797
OR 1-602-297-8200

Order Form Key
TB37BP

Useful Finishing Sources

Architectural Antiques Exchange
715 N. Second St.
Philadelphia, PA 19123
(215) 922-3669
FAX (215) 922-3680
doors, entryways, etched glass, fencing &
gates, windows

Anthony Wood Products, Inc.
P.O. Box 1081
Hillsboro, TX 76645
(817) 582-7225
FAX (817) 582-7620
arches, balusters, brackets, corbels, drops,
finials, fretwork, gable trim, spindles

The Balmer Architectural Art Studios
9 Codeco Ct.
Don Mills, ONT M3A 1B6 Canada
(416) 449-2155
FAX (416) 449-3098
cartouches, centerpieces, festoons, finials,
friezes, keystones, medallions, mouldings,
pilasters, rosettes

Blue Ox Millworks
Foot of X St.
Eureka, CA 95501
(800) 248-4259 (707) 444-3437
FAX (707) 444-0918
balusters, basemboards, door & window
casings, gutters, mouldings, porches, posts,
vergeboards, wainscoting

Cain Architectural Art Glass
Rt. 1 Box AAA
Bremo Bluff, VA 23022
(804) 842-3984
beveled glass, windows, custom beveling on
traditional machinery

Classic Architectural Specialties
3223 Canton St.
Dallas TX 75226
(214) 748-1668 (in Dallas)
(800) 622-1221
FAX (214) 748-7149
uncommon architectural features

Creative Openings
P.O. Box 4204
Bellingham, WA 98227
(800) 677-6420 (206) 671-6420
screen doors

Cumberland Woodcraft Co.
P.O. Drawer 609
Carlisle, PA 17013
(800) 367-1884 (outside of PA)
(717) 243-0063
FAX (717) 243-6502
balusters, brackets, carvings, corbels, doors,
fretwork, mouldings, screen doors

Custom Ironwork, Inc.
P.O. Box 180
Union, KY 41091
(606) 384-4122
FAX (606) 384-4848
fencing & gates, furniture

Denninger Cupolas & Weathervanes
RD 1, Box 447
Middletown, NY 10940
(914) 343-2229
cupolas

Elegant Entries
240 Washington St.
Auburn, MA 01501
(800) 343-3432
(508) 832-9898 (in MA)
FAX (508) 832-6874
beveled glass, doors, art glass

Fancy Front Brassiere Co.
P.O. Box 2847
Roseville, CA 95746
(916) 791-7733
FAX (916) 773-2956
balusters, brackets, corbels, gable trim,
posts, screen doors

Focal Point Inc.
P.O. Box 93327
Atlanta, GA 30377-0327
(800) 662-5550 (404) 351-0820
arches, centerpieces, door & window casings,
entryways, festoons, friezes, keystones,
medallions, mouldings, rosettes

Gothom, Inc.
Box 421, 110 Main St.
Erin, ONT N0B 1T0 Canada
(519) 833-2574 FAX (519) 833-9751
balusters, porches, posts, screen doors,
vergeboards

Hicksville Woodworks Co.
265 Jerusalem Ave.
Hicksville, NY 11801
(516) 938-0171
arches, balusters, fencing & gates, finials,
vergeboards

Mad River Woodworks Co.
Box 1067
Blue Lake, CA 95525-1067
(707) 668-5671
brackets, drops, entryways, finials,
mouldings, posts, spandrels, wainscoting

W.F. Norman Corporation
P.O. Box 323, 214 N. Cedar
Nevada, MO 64772-0323
(800) 641-4038 (417) 667-5552
FAX (417) 667-2708
balusters, brackets, cartouches, finials,
friezes, keystones, mouldings

The Old Wagon Factory
P.O. Box 1427, Dept. PHE91
Clarksville, VA 23927
(804) 374-5787
storm screens

Ornamental Mouldings Limited
P.O. Box 336
Waterloo, ONT N2J 4A4 Canada
(519) 884-4080
FAX (519) 884-9692
in the United States:
P.O. Box 7123
High Point, NC 27264
baseboards, door & window casings,
mouldings

The Renovators Supply
P100 Renovators Old Mill
Millers Falls, MA 01349
(413) 659-2211 (413) 659-2241
FAX (413) 659-3976
classic hardware, plumbing, lighting and
home decorating items

San Francisco Victoriana, Inc.
2070 Newcomb Ave.
San Francisco, CA 94124
(415) 648-0313
FAX (415) 648-2812
baseboards, brackets, centerpieces, door &
window casings, festoons, medallions,
mouldings, pilasters, posts, rosettes,
wainscoting

Silverton Victorian Millworks
P.O. Box 2987 - HPI
Durango, CO 81302
(800) 933-3930 (303) 259-5915
FAX (303) 259-5919
arches, balusters, baseboards, brackets,
carvings, door and window casings, drops,
keystones, mouldings, pilasters, porches,
posts, screen doors, vergeboards,
wainscoting, windows

Tennessee Fabricating Co.
2025 York Ave.
Memphis, TN 38104
(901) 725-1548
brackets, fencing & gates, finials, porches

Vintage Wood Works
Highway 34
P.O. Box R
Quinlan, TX 75474
(903) 356-2158
arches, balusters, brackets, corbels, drops,
finials, fretwork, gable decorations, porches,
posts, spandrels, vergeboards

Wood Factory
901 Harvard
Houston, TX 77008
(713) 863-7600 FAX (713) 863-1183
corbels, doors, gables, mouldings